W9-AUZ-300

Also by Jessica B. Harris

Beyond Gumbo

The Africa Cookbook

The Welcome Table

A Kwanzaa Keepsake

Tasting Brazil

Sky Juice & Flying Fish

Iron Pots & Wooden Spoons

Hot Stuff

The Black Family Reunion Cookbook
  (*with The National Council of Negro Women*)

SIMON & SCHUSTER • New York London Toronto Sydney

ON THE SIDE

More Than 100 Recipes for the Sides,
Salads, and Condiments that
Make the Meal

JESSICA B. HARRIS

SIMON & SCHUSTER
Rockefeller Center
1230 Avenue of the Americas
New York, NY 10020

SIMON & SCHUSTER and colophon are registered trademarks
of Simon & Schuster, Inc.

For information about special discounts for bulk purchases,
please contact Simon & Schuster Special Sales:
1-800-456-6798 or business@simonandschuster.com

Book design by Ellen R. Sasahara

Manufactured in the United States of America

10   9   8   7   6   5   4   3   2   1

Library of Congress Cataloging-in-Publication Data
Harris, Jessica B.
   On the side : more than 100 recipes for the sides, salads,
      and condiments that make the meal. / Jessica B. Harris.
   p. cm.
   Includes Index.
   1. Side dishes (Cookery). I. Title.
TX801.H33 2004
641.8'—dc22
              2004045375

ISBN 0-7432-4917-8

Dedication

To my Parents, always,

And to my international second and third generations
from Bahia and Benin, London and Louisiana, and beyond.

They join hands across continents and oceans and spangle the universe with
their shimmering delight in being as they unite the world with music and
dance, laughter, love, and food.

May the world that they are creating be a better place for us all.

Acknowledgments

A luta continua. Thanks go to my world that continues to keep me alive and on the planet and who insists daily that I tell the story well. First among them are Cheikh Oumar Thiam, Kerry Moody, Audreen Buffalo, Liv and Willy Blumer, Lolis Eric Elie, Dolly McPherson, Maya Angelou, Mammadou Sy, Gail and Birch McDonough, Lou and Mary Len Costa, Michele and Ulrick Jean Pierre, Alexander Smalls, Mitzi Pratt, John Martin Taylor, Mikey, Kit, and the Charleston crew, Patricia Hopkins, Lucille Rich, Daphne Derven, Maria Williams-Jones, Martha Jones, Carey Pickard, Keren Tonneson, Martha Taylor, Maryse Pochot, Chester Higgins and Betsey Kissam, Trish and Tony Garnier, Matt and Anne Konigsmark and baby Gus, Fritz Blank, Marcella Martinez, the Elie family, Claire Bersani and Mahmoud Mussawish, Pat Lawrence and Noel, Simon and Shelly Gunning, Jan Brady and John Batty, Patrick Dunne and the staff at Lucullus, Carol Cadogan, Carole Abel, Judy Kern, Olive Tomlinson, Gretchen Tucker-Underwood, Charlayne Hunter-Gault and family, Kate Dyson and family in London, Betty Fussell, Bette Weidman, Ralph Taylor, Monty Cumberbatch, Nello Bynoe and all at Almond Resorts, Mae Tata and my sisters and brothers at Casa Branca in Bahia, especially Sinha and her sons, and Theophile and Theodora, Aimee and Albert, and the members of my African Komaclo/Houemavo/Grimaud family.

Then, there are folks along the journey who have become friends who also give me strength and keep me moving forward. Andrew Hopkins, Jinx and Jeff Morgan, Don Richmond, Dennis Greene, Linda Mayo-Perez, Matt Rowley, Suzie Segal, Ron and Nancy Harrell, Myrna Colley Lee and Morgan, Ron and Troy Bechet, Anna Rita and John Scott, Phillip Collins, Kim Dummons, Ann Wilder, John T. Edge, Blair, Jesse, Dorothy and Tom

Howorth, Jan Arnow and family, and the numerous members of my very personal international rainbow tribe.

Now, there is a second generation: Funsho Allu, Gersoney d'Azevedo, Leonora Costa, Alexandre Grimaud and family, Christian Grimaud and family, Kamau Bobb and family, Jennifer and Bruce Pochot, Charles Anthony and Jani'e, Kym, Carla, Jack, Serge, Hadja, Abdoulaye, Ousmane, Tsede, and all those who call me "Auntie" and remind me with their caring, their curiosity, and their love that I write to pass it on.

There are the friends in the world of food who have fed me literally and spiritually, allowed me to ask stupid questions, and sometimes even play in their kitchens, and even treated me as an equal. Thanks to Leah Chase, Patricia Wilson, Robert Oliver, Ken Smith, JoAnn Clevenger, Ariane Daguin, Paul Hamilton, William Woys Weaver, Fatema Hal, Michelle Nugent, Poppy Tooker, Julie Sahni, Carmelita Jeanne, Karen Hess, Te, John Currence, Jasper White and all the folks at Jasper's Summer Shack, Mark Miller, the gang at Sterling Rice, and all of the folks at the Southern Foodways Alliance.

Thanks are also due to librarians, booksellers, and antiquarian book dealers too numerous to note who feed my obsession and continue to fill my head with thoughts and my shelves with books.

Daily the QC lunch bunch makes me laugh; Ron Cottman keeps the rain off and the furnace chugging. From Mr. Wright to M. Pierre a wondrous succession of taxi drivers gets me where I'm going, and my neighbors—Monica Payne-Hall, Lance Hall, Amad, Julia, and Avery—gracefully smile at my shortcomings, and feed my cats and water my plants when I'm out of town.

Finally, these efforts would not be a book without the on-going ministrations and attentions of my ever-encouraging and always patient agent, Susan Ginsburg, and her assistant, Rachel; my long-suffering editor, Sydny Miner, with whom I have worked for longer than many of my friends have been married, her assistant, Laura Holmes, and the entire publication staff at Simon & Schuster who continue to treat me as though I wore a crown.

To all of you and to the ones whom I inadvertently forgot, my gratitude is as deeply heartfelt as it is endless.

The ultimate thanks go to God, the Orisha, and the creative spirits who gave me the parents I try to honor with my work, the brain I try to challenge at each turn, and the joy of being me in the world. I am grateful.

Contents

A FEW WORDS ON THE SIDE

Sides make the meal. Most of the color, taste, and variety of a meal come from their presence. It's impossible to imagine the Thanksgiving turkey without the trimmings of candied sweet potatoes, creamed onions, cranberry sauce, and the individual additions that each family brings. A New England clambake without the corn and potatoes is simply clams and lobster. Even a humble hamburger reverts to a slab of chopped meat without the coleslaw, lettuce, tomato, and pickle (not to mention the mustard, ketchup, and relish!).

In restaurants, it often seems that tiny elfin hands have labored until each plate looks like an Arcimboldo still life and there are few separate side dishes. In the home kitchen, things are different. Sides rule! They transform the mundane into the magnificent and round out the meal.

In my twenty-five years of writing about food and my fifty-six-plus years of eating it, I must confess that while I am a confirmed carnivore and adore fish and poultry, what really keeps me going is an overwhelming desire to eat the food to the side of the protein. This book is the result of that love. It is also the result of decades of collecting interesting and innovative side dishes from around the world that are simple and flavorful. These are honest dishes that may be as simple as a new twist on string beans that I picked up in a Paris kitchen, or a North African way with tomatoes, or a Brazilian hot sauce that adds extra zest to sautéed greens. Some recipes are from my family and friends, others are variations on international classics which I developed during my nightly adventures in the kitchen, and still others come from my travels around the world researching culinary history. They all are simple to prepare and they add zest and color to the plate, vibrancy to the meal, and most important, flavor to the table.

Vegetable side dishes in the European tradition, though, are not always a part of other culinary traditions. Side dishes may come to the diner as snacks, as road food, or even as a meatless main dish. I've taken the liberty here of using the European format of service and calling the seasonal selection of vegetable dishes sides.

Salads range from the simple green salad to a pull-out-all-of-the-stops potato salad complete with olives and dill pickles. Again, salads are not always served as a separate course in other cultures, if they come to the table at all. They can appear at virtually any place in the meal from beginning to end.

There's no such problem with condiments. Here, world dining traditions offer a range of relishes and pickles, salsas and chutneys, hot sauces, mustards, ketchups, and more.

Each of the book's five chapters begins with its own presentation of the sides discussed, so read straight through or flip and skip. When you are finally ready to cook, turn to "A Few Notes on Ingredients" on page 5, as well as to "Mail-Order Sources" on page 201, for advice on choosing and finding ingredients. Whether you're a partisan of the tastefully mild or delight in the astonishingly piquant, you're sure to find something that will allow you to have just a little bit more on the side.

New York, New Orleans, and Oak Bluffs,
August 2003

Chapter 1

SEASONAL SIDES

When I was in grade school, we delighted in singing a song by the British satirists Flanders and Swann that began, "January brings the snow, makes your feet and fingers glow." The song continued through the months highlighting all of the madness of the yearly cycle and then ended with the words, "Freezing wet December then, Bloody January again!"

The cycle of the year does have a repetitive quality, but I love the change of seasons. Increasingly, I find that my love of food follows a seasonal calendar as well, one based in the three cardinal points of my personal compass: New York, New Orleans, and Martha's Vineyard. My calendar follows the changing produce in the various farmers' markets, whether they're located on Union Square or Grand Army Plaza, on Magazine Street, at the old French Market at the edge of the *Vieux Carré,* in Chilmark near the old agricultural hall, or anywhere I'm traveling in the world. It seems that year-round I'm in one or another of them sniffing tomatoes, thumping melons, and trying to discover something new and wonderful as I continue to look for something to serve on the side.

I visit and have visited many of the world's markets, and I cook lots of the dishes I learned in them. When I think of seasons and markets, I think of my first trips to Europe and the delight I took in recognizing that the Old World knew better than to trust its provisioning to plain old supermarkets. The Marché du Buci, the Marché de Neuilly, and the market on the rue Mouffetard in Paris were the sites of many an early culinary epiphany. In later years, I'd travel farther afield. The swirl of saris in Madras, India, as women haggled over hairy brown coconuts and the brilliant pink turbans that occasionally turned up on Rajasthani vendors selling carrots so orange they were almost red are vivid memories. These recollections mix with the images of shoppers and tastes of new vegetables found in markets on the subcontinent and in Hong Kong, Singapore, and Penang.

I also think of my many treks ankle-deep in aromatic mud in the markets of West Africa. I recall the flower women of Dakar's Kermel Market, and the special-for-European-expatriates vegetables that contrasted so vividly with the more robust fare of the Marché Sandaga and the meager offerings of the Marché Tilène and the Marché du H.L.M. I think back to the glory days of the Côte d'Ivoire when the Marché du Treichville exploded with produce from the Sahel and the forest: gigantic snails nestled in their effluvia a few steps away from tempting pineapples that perfumed the air. There, in the Abidjan of years gone by, the Marché de Cocody was the one for the expats, and in season you could find *haricots verts* and avocados that were firm and ripe and almost too good to eat. In Cotonou, I waited with anticipation for the five-day schedule to yield another market day, so that I could pester my friends to take me once again to the Dan Tokpa, the mother of all West African markets. I remember darkened alleyways in Mombasa and bright farm stands in Capetown, each with its own specialties and its own ambiance.

In this hemisphere, there are almost too many favorites to note. In Jamaica, there's the small oh-so-nontouristy market down a side street in Montego Bay where I tasted sugar loaf pineapples for the first time and met one amazingly sassy market woman. Martinique boasts a market in Fort-de-France that dates back to Eiffel, where the sellers of pickles and tropical fruit syrups ply their trade. Barbados's market is small and drab in comparison, but the market women are no less feisty.

Belém's Ver-O-Paso in Brazil has everything from *pirarucú* fish to tropical fruits galore to brilliant parrots, but it can't compete with the Mercado São Joaquim in Bahia for tastes of dendê and cassava meal, and even that one takes a back seat to the Saturday market in the tiny outlying town of Cachoeira.

All of the markets of my world share a sense of community and celebrate the continuity of folks bantering, catching up on the week's events and gossip while purchasing the things they'll need to place meals on the table for the coming days. It's the same in New York.

New York is home base, so I see the season run from asparagus and new potatoes in spring, through the last Brussels sprouts and turnips, to the Christmas wreaths and trees of the final markets before it all begins again. In New York I walk more rapidly but still savor the camaraderie of the market that is the city's equivalent of the friendly banter that happens in markets all over the world.

I love people-watching, from the dreadlocked Rastas stocking up on organic veggies for Ital meals and young couples planning romantic bouts of cooking *à deux,* to sandal-wearing daddies with babies on their chests and knapsacks bulging with produce on their backs. They, like their colleagues around the world, celebrate the seasonality of food, savor the freshest of ingredients, and revel in the moment of the agora—the market or meeting place.

When my mother died, shortly after midnight on May 20, 2000, I was devastated: lost and without anchor. I knew only that it was a Saturday morning and, after a sorrow-filled trip to my empty childhood home, I asked my friend to take me to the farmers' market on Grand Army Plaza, the one nearest to my house. There, amid the bustle and the vegetables, I centered myself. I knew markets had always been important to me, but I never in my wildest imaginings thought that the flurry of the quotidian would help me find solace on what was the worst day of my life. Yet I wandered the stalls, poking here, pinching there, and I found peace and somehow the will to continue. I looked around and realized that life *does* go on. I shopped and recovered myself and returned home able to cope with events and deal with my grief, and also with flowers, fruit, and food to cook for myself and others. Since my mother's death, I acknowledge my connection to and love of markets. The markets and farmers' markets at home and abroad with their seasonal cycle have became anchors of my life.

In New Orleans, I snag a ride with one of my early-rising friends and we head off to see what the farmers' market on Magazine Street has to offer. I still haven't got the dates right for when to expect Lionel Keyes and the handmade filé he pounds in the old mortar that he inherited from his Uncle Bill. But I know that at some point he'll appear, as will the gentleman who sells his small piles of heirloom chillies that have been arranged chromatically. There are newcomers, like the wheatgrass man who always seems to run out of his spicy apple juice just before I arrive, and old hands, like the ladies selling greens and the ever-ebullient woman who cheerfully extolls the virtues of her preserves and pickles to all who will listen. The lavender folks with their flower sprigs and wonderful honey and the sugar cane man with his dark syrup and wondrous vinegar appear seasonally, and I'm always pleased to see their return. I know that the strawberries will usually turn up in April, the Creole tomatoes arrive in June, and the citrus season that brings tangerine-like satsumas comes near Christmas. That's the time of year I make a trip across the river to Bechnel's for bags of satsumas as well as blood oranges and grapefruit to haul back to New York.

The garden folks are there year round and I can never resist their small pots of herbs. I'm always trying to squeeze another rooting of verbena, lavender, or rosemary into my small, crowded garden where I insist on a plot of kitchen herbs. There's already a 10-foot-tall bay tree as well as the bird chillies and rosemary that were part of my reason for buying the house, but my list of must-have herbs keeps growing. I delight in their fragrance each morning in the Crescent City before I snip and pull them in the afternoon as I begin to cook.

Martha's Vineyard means summer and in those months I write books, test recipes on willing friends, and commune with my family ghosts in the house my parents purchased over forty-five years ago. As a true born-and-bred New Yorker I don't drive, so I never refuse a ride up-island on Wednesday or Saturday to head to the farmers' market in Chilmark. There, I watch as the few tables from early July selling baked goods and the last tomato and pepper plants for setting outside and the greens from Whippoorwill Farm that I dream about the rest of the year blossom into a visual and gustatory cornucopia of produce.

By mid-August it's in full swing complete with tiny potato "culls" and heirloom tomatoes, fresh and dried herbs of every variety, homemade goods like pineapple salsas and savory focaccias, zucchini and their blossoms and even, occasionally, special items like tomatillos. The island sweet corn—the butter and sugar yellow and white variety—is dangerously habit-forming as are the homemade lemonade and ginger ale that my friend, Heidi, sometimes sells. The crowd is eclectic: Oak Bluffs flash meets Edgartown sedate, Aquinnah's earth mothers commune with West Tisbury's intelligentsia, and there are enough black and golden labs nosing their way through the crowd to make any canine lover happy. We all cheerfully poke and prod and gossip, and meet and greet the folks we haven't seen in a year, then leave for home with baskets laden with produce and accented by bunches of zinnias and sunflowers.

Too soon, the pumpkins appear and signal that it's time to think of home and with a few tomatoes for the road and a pumpkin or two to hold me until Halloween, I head back to New York's markets for the final tomatoes and okra of the season and the first Brussels sprouts that tell me that my culinary year has come full circle yet again.

A Few Notes on Ingredients

Throughout the recipes there are some ingredients used repeatedly that are not always specified by type. So unless noted otherwise, when a recipe calls for butter, you should use salted; for onions, yellow globe; for parsley, regular curly parsley; and for pepper, freshly ground black peppercorns (I like Tellicherry). I use fine sea salt and Diamond Crystal interchangeably, unless something else is called for. Chillies should be treated with care (see page 120); they don't need to be seeded unless the recipe asks for seeded chilies, or you want to lower the heat.

SEASONAL SIDES

SUMMER

YEAR-ROUND FAVORITES

FALL

I am a child of the colder months. Perhaps it's the eighteen-plus years of attending school, or the additional thirty-four-plus years of teaching, but my years seem to follow an academic calendar. Oh sure, I celebrate New Year's Day with Hoppin' John and collard greens, but for me Labor Day takes on all of the solemnity of New Year's, for this is in truth when my year begins. After my lengthy academic summer vacation, I still retain a childish glee at the acquisition of new school supplies, and I'm secretly excited to see what the next class of students will bring.

One of the things I delight in most in the fall is the return of heartier foods to my menu after summer's salads. It's a season of saying farewell to some of my summer favorites—the corn and tomatoes and tiny pods of okra—and hello to the leeks and cauliflower and celeriac that will signal the return of the colder months.

Fall Favorite Vegetables

Long Beans or Yard-Long Beans
(Vigna unguiculata, var. sesquipedalis)

Although they are used in manner similar to the more familiar green beans, snap beans, and string beans, long beans are actually a relative of the black-eyed pea. If allowed to mature, they will produce a pea similar to their more common cousin. They grow on a climbing plant that can reach thirteen feet in height. The beans are thought to have originated in Africa and spread from there to India and China, and then to the Mediterranean and the New World. They are popular in the food of the Caribbean where they are called *bora* or *boonchi* or *bodi* in Guyana, Aruba, and Trinidad, respectively.

They are either deep or light green in color and look like very long green beans; each bean may be from one to three feet long. The taste, though, is different; yard-long beans have a denser, richer flavor than green beans. Instead of a crunch, they develop an almost velvety texture. They're also known as asparagus bean, which gives another hint to their flavor.

When purchasing long beans, look for beans that are not too thick and whose the seeds or peas are not overdeveloped. They're quite fragile and don't keep well, so purchase them as you need them and use them quickly. Long beans can be found in most Caribbean and Asian markets.

Brussels Sprouts
(Brassica oleracea, Gemmifera Group)

Looking like tiny cabbages on a stem, Brussels sprouts begin to turn up in my favorite farmers' markets in the fall and I am always quick to snag some. Brussels sprouts first became popular in England and France in home gardens around the end of the eighteenth century. By 1812 Thomas Jefferson recorded planting the sprouts in his gardens at Monticello.

They've become a ubiquitous fall and winter vegetable, but all too often are overcooked and mushy, or too mature and too cabbage-y in taste. Chef Robbin Hass in Florida removes the leaves from each tiny sprout, steams them lightly, and then reassembles the leaves in a gently tossed pile. It's a great thing to try when you've got lots of time and many hands.

Purchase sprouts while they're young and tender; they should be bright green with no yellowing. They'll keep for three to four days in the refrigerator. The real trick is in the cooking. Remember, don't overcook them!

Cauliflower
(Brassica oleracea, Botrytis Group)

Although cauliflower is as common as carrots and readily available at your local grocery store virtually all year round, this relative of the broccoli plant has an exotic lineage. Some think that it originated in the Near East; others opt for an African origin and suggest that Egyptians cultivated the plant as early as the fourth century B.C. Introduced by the Arabs to Europe after the fall of the

Roman Empire, cauliflower reached France in the mid-sixteenth century. From there cauliflower made its way to northern Europe and to the United States.

Cauliflower is actually a head of undeveloped flower buds attached to a central stalk. The familiar white head or curd is produced by covering it from the sun, thereby blanching it. Leaving it uncovered will result in other colors ranging from yellow to green to deep purple.

Cauliflower should be purchased when it is white and shows no blemishes or brown spots, and the leaves should be a bright green. If not, it's too old! Cauliflower can be kept in the refrigerator for a little over a week.

Celery Root or Celeriac

(Apium graveolens, var. rapaceum)

This knobby turnip-sized root is immensely popular in France, where it is the basis for *céleri rémoulade.* The root comes into its own in the cooler months; it has a creamy flesh that can be grated and eaten raw or cooked and puréed or braised and served solo or with other vegetables. It tastes richly of celery.

Celeriac is increasingly available at markets. Look for firm, heavy roots that are relatively regular in shape. (The shape has nothing to do with taste, but will make the root easier to peel.) Select smaller roots over larger, as the bigger ones tend to become woody. The root will keep well for several weeks in the refrigerator. Sprinkle the surface with lemon juice or vinegar after cutting it as it will darken on contact with the air.

Leeks

(Allium porrum)

Leeks are not just overgrown scallions, and they're good for more than vichyssoise. Although mentioned in the Bible and cultivated by the ancient Egyptians, no one is sure where the plant originated. Leeks are the symbol of Wales in the United Kingdom and are mentioned as such in Shakespeare's *Henry V.*

Leeks should be purchased when they are firm with bright green tops. They will keep for up to two weeks in the refrigerator; they can also be stored like onions in a cool damp place for about two months. The trouble with leeks, as anyone who has cooked them knows, is not in the selection but in the cleaning. They are grown in dirt and inevitably bring more of it to market than necessary. The trick is to remove the root end and the outer leaves, trim the green tops and then slit them lengthwise at least once. Then wash them, wash them, and wash them again.

Okra

(Abelmosschus esculentus or Hibiscus esculentus)

Okra originated in Africa, either in Western Africa or in the Horn of Africa near Ethiopia and from there it migrated to northern Africa and the rest of the world. It arrived in the United States to feed enslaved Africans. We get our word okra from the Twi language of Ghana; the word by which it is known in much of the rest of the world—*gombo*—comes from the Bantu languages of Central Africa. It's called *gingambo* in Puerto Rico and Cuba, *quiabo* in Brazil, *malondron* in the Dominican Republic, *bamia* or *bamya* in Egypt, *bhindi* in India, and lady's fingers in much of the English speaking world. It's eaten in all of those places with much relish.

In the United States it remains, sadly, a dish prized mainly by Southerners and African-Americans, as others don't like its slippery mouth-feel. It's wonderful as a thickener—just witness the gumbos of Southern Louisiana and the okra soups of Charleston. Okra is not at all slimy when breaded with cornmeal and fried; it can be blanched and served as a salad, and it's even eaten raw. To lovers of the pod, it's nigh unto perfect in the southern summer succotashes of okra, corn, and tomatoes.

Okra is best when purchased young. Select small, unblemished pods without any black markings or soft spots. Okra does not keep well and should be kept dry and only for a few days in the refrigerator. A final word: the more you cut okra, the more mucilaginous it becomes, so cook accordingly. I've said that wherever okra points its green tip Africa has passed. That's why I have a picture of it on my business card and on my stationery.

Tumis Buncis

Indonesian-style Green Beans   *Serves 4 to 6*

This is a classic Indonesian dish, usually prepared with string beans. However, for a slightly different version, I've used more exotic long beans. The denser, silkier texture of the long beans adds another fillip to the dish. If you can't find long beans—available in Caribbean markets under the name of *bora* and as "long beans" in Chinese and Asian markets—just use regular string beans.

1¼ pounds long beans
2 fresh red chiltecpin chillies, or to taste
2 tablespoons vegetable oil
3 shallots, peeled and thinly sliced
2 cloves garlic, thinly sliced
1 teaspoon ground ginger
Pinch of freshly grated nutmeg
Salt and freshly ground black pepper, to taste
¼ cup chicken stock

Top and tail the beans and cut them diagonally into 2-inch pieces. Stem and seed the chillies and cut them diagonally into 1-inch pieces. Heat the oil in a wok and add the shallots, garlic, ginger, nutmeg, and salt and pepper, and stir-fry for about 1 minute. Add the beans and chillies and continue to stir-fry for an additional 2 minutes. Add the stock, cover, and reduce the heat. Simmer for 5 minutes, or until the beans are al dente but fork-tender. Correct the seasonings and serve hot.

Braised Celery Root   *Serves 4*

I first came across celery root (also known as celeriac) in France where it is the basis for *céleri rémoulade,* one of the salads that was always included in plates of hors d'oeuvres in years gone by. Back then, celery root was hard to find in the United States, but now with our increasing repertoire of ingredients, it's readily available and at its best in the fall. When made into dishes like this, braised celery root brings a different taste to the table in the fall and winter months.

1½ pounds (1 medium) celery root
Salt (for blanching)
1 tablespoon olive oil
1 tablespoon unsalted butter
1 bay leaf
1 small onion, minced
Salt and freshly ground black pepper, to taste
½ cup chicken stock (you could also use turkey or vegetable stock)
¼ cup dry white wine
Minced flat-leaf parsley for garnish

Preheat the oven to 350 degrees. Wash the celery root, peel it, and cut it into ½-inch slices. Blanch the slices for 10 minutes in salted boiling water. Remove and drain. Heat the olive oil and butter in a flameproof casserole, add the bay leaf and minced onion, and cook until the onion is tender but not brown. Add the drained celery root slices and allow them to brown for a few minutes on both sides. Season to taste with salt and pepper. Add the chicken stock and wine and bring to a boil. Remove from the heat, place the dish in the oven, and bake uncovered for approximately 25 minutes, or until the celery root is tender. Strain the remaining juices into a small saucepan, and bring to a boil. Then lower the heat and continue to cook until the volume is reduced by half. Serve the reduced juices as a sauce over the hot celery root. Garnish with minced parsley.

Bamia Masloukah
Egyptian-style Okra   *Serves 6*

Okra is a vegetable witness of the African Diaspora, and is eaten all over the world. Many African-Americans cling to it with ferocious tenacity. We eat it during the summer when it is young and into the fall when it is getting more mature. During the months when it is unavailable fresh, we eat okra pickles and might even resort to frozen or, Lord forbid, canned okra. This is an Egyptian way with okra.

1½ pounds small okra pods
1 tablespoon olive oil
1 medium onion, minced
2 cups beef stock
1 teaspoon freshly squeezed lemon juice

Wash the okra and top it, discarding any blemished or hard pods. Heat the oil in a heavy saucepan, add the onion, and sauté until translucent. Add the okra and cook for 3 minutes, stirring constantly. Add the stock, cover, and cook for an additional 5 to 7 minutes, or until the okra is tender. Add the lemon juice and serve hot.

Cauliflower *Serves 4 to 6*

Like most Americans, I grew up eating cauliflower. Broken into little florets, it made an annual appearance on the table during the fall and winter months alternating with broccoli. I was never aware of the elegant possibilities of this cabbage relative until it was served to me by Mary Garin, the wife of a starred Michelin chef. There, in their Paris apartment, she served the entire head of cauliflower that had been cooked to tender, alabaster perfection. The head was elegant, presented in its entirety, complete with a few of the tender green leaves at the bottom. She served simple drawn butter to drizzle over it and a grating of fresh nutmeg to bring out the flavor.

1 head cauliflower, with most of the outside leaves removed
4 tablespoons melted butter, or to taste
Salt and freshly grated nutmeg, to taste

Bring water to a boil in a large, deep saucepan big enough to hold the entire head of cauliflower. Gently place the cauliflower into the boiling water, cover, and cook for 10 to 15 minutes or until crisp-tender. Remove, drain, and serve immediately, topped with a drizzle of the butter, a sprinkling of salt, and a grating or two of fresh nutmeg.

Leeks with Lemon Butter   *Serves 4 to 6*

Many people ignore leeks when they see them, either because they're not sure how to prepare them, or because they know just how much grit can be packed inside those white bulbs. I've learned to love leeks and in the winter I often prepare a quick soup of leeks, white potatoes, bouillon cubes, and milk. In the fall, I serve them with a lemon butter to which I add a chiffonade of the last of the lemon verbena that I bring up from New Orleans.

2 tablespoons extra virgin olive oil
5 tablespoons unsalted butter
6 to 8 leeks, trimmed, quartered, and scrupulously cleaned
½ cup chicken stock
1 tablespoon freshly squeezed lemon juice
1 teaspoon minced lemon verbena leaves
Salt and freshly ground black pepper, to taste

Heat the olive oil and 3 tablespoons of the butter in a heavy skillet. Add the well-cleaned leeks and sauté them over medium heat for about 5 minutes. Add the chicken stock and reduce the heat. Simmer for about 15 minutes, or until the leeks are fork-tender but not mushy. Drain the leeks and place them on a heated serving platter. While the leeks are braising, melt the remaining 2 tablespoons of butter in a small saucepan with the lemon juice and lemon verbena. Season with salt and pepper and pour it over the leeks. Serve hot.

Brussels Sprouts and Chestnuts *Serves 6 to 8*

I love the cruciferous vegetables that begin to come into their own in the fall. I tend to cook a big bunch of Brussels sprouts at once and then stir-fry the leftovers with garlic for the next day's meal. The first night, though, is reserved for Brussels sprouts and chestnuts, my idea of a perfect fall food combination.

1 pound Brussels sprouts
1 pound chestnuts (in the shell)
Salt and freshly ground black pepper, to taste

Wash the Brussels sprouts, pare off any blemished parts, and cut an X into the stem ends. Place them in a saucepan with water to cover and bring to a boil. Lower the heat and cook for 8 minutes, or until fork-tender.

Cut an X into the rounded side of the chestnuts with a chestnut knife, place them in another pot of boiling water, and cook for about 15 minutes. Drain and remove the shell and inner skin while the chestnuts are still warm. Combine both vegetables in a serving dish, season to taste, and serve hot.

WINTER

With a March birthday, I am a child of the winter months. I love to hibernate in the winter, taking my cues from the bears. I luxuriate in doing homebound things. I delight in the clear days when the sun shines and the air is crisp with a hint of snow.

Winter is when I return to the comfort foods of my youth and re-create side dishes from the vegetables that my mother prepared while I was growing up. I spend winter reclaiming my roots, literally, as most of the vegetables that go into my winter pot are root vegetables, perfect for the hearty dishes that the season calls for.

Favorite Winter Vegetables

Cabbage
(Brassica oleracea)

Although cabbage is widely used in the cooking of Northern Europe, most believe that it originated in the Middle East. It grows wild there and a non-heading form was eaten by the ancient Egyptians, much like the collard greens of the American South. They thought that eating raw cabbage would keep one from becoming drunk. The Greeks also knew the vegetable in a non-heading form. The Romans brought cabbage to Britain and northern Europe where it quickly became a staple. From sauerkraut to kimchi, the vegetable is used in pickles and to prepare hearty dishes. In the warmer regions, cabbage is also used, often curried.

Cabbage is readily available; look for heads that are heavy and tightly closed. The leaves should be unblemished and not have any tears or dark spots. Cabbage can be stored for about two weeks in the refrigerator, but beware: it will begin to have a cabbage-y smell which it will gladly share with all the other items nearby if it is not well wrapped.

Parsnips

(Pastinaca sativa)

This root looks like a white carrot. Parsnips have an ancient history and were widely used in Europe before the Columbian exchange brought the potato from the New World. Parsnips are sweeter than many carrots and have an underlying hint of celery to which they are also related. Early writers didn't really distinguish between parsnips and carrots and used the term parsnip to refer to both. Like collard greens, parsnips are improved by frost and are a cold weather vegetable par excellence.

Parsnips are increasingly available in supermarkets and farmers' markets. Select ones that are uniform in size and not too large, as the larger ones may be woody. They can be kept refrigerated for up to a month. Prepare parsnips the same way as carrots, but if they're going to be kept after cutting and before cooking, they need a bit of lemon juice or vinegar water to keep them from discoloring.

Potatoes

(Solanum tubersum)

Potatoes were one of the vegetables that Columbus unleashed on the unsuspecting world. These natives of the Andean regions of South America had been cultivated there for more than 6,000 years before his arrival. In South America, there are so many varieties of potatoes that some Andean markets fairly bulge with stalls selling varieties in multiple hues of red, purple, brown, yellow, black, and blue.

The potato was one of Columbus's success stories and was taken to the heart of Europe with a vengeance. Expect for a short period during the seventeenth century when the poor old spud was thought to cause leprosy, the potato became a replacement for bread in some parts of Europe, or at least its accompaniment. Parts of Europe, in fact, became overly dependent on the potato. When the crops failed in Ireland in 1845 and 1846, the resulting Irish potato famine brought hundreds of Irish immigrants, and their love of the spud, to the United States. Potatoes, which had already been introduced from the West Indies in the seventeenth century, became even more popular.

Potatoes are readily available and even some of the trendier cultivars can be had at almost any supermarket. Some potatoes can be kept for several months but a good rule of thumb is to buy only what you need. Look for firm potatoes with no sprouts.

Rutabagas
(Brassica Napus, Napobrassica Group)

Rutabagas, also known as swedes, are a cross between the turnip and the savoy cabbage that was developed in Scandinavia in the Middle Ages. Introduced in the United States in the nineteenth century, they have been the subject of many a culinary joke since then. I guess my mother's family was different, or perhaps too poor to avoid the root. I grew up loving its nutty taste.

Rutabagas are in most supermarkets and you've probably walked by them time and time again. Rutabagas are the large purplish-orange root that's often next to the turnips. They're usually waxed for longer shelf life and must be peeled before use. Select rutabagas that are firm, heavy, and without blemishes or soft spots. They will keep in the refrigerator for up to three weeks.

Sweet Potatoes
(Ipomea batatas)

The sweet potato is the subject of much culinary confusion created by Africans in the diaspora. This New World root vegetable is often called by the name of the African root it most resembles—the yam—a misidentification that makes botanists cringe. Sweet potatoes are New World species that originated in Central America and northern South America while yams are something entirely different.

Sweet potatoes are not potatoes either; they're actually related to morning glories. They're old tubers. Remains of sweet potatoes that date back over 12,000 years have been discovered in a cave in Peru. While we in the United States are very familiar with the orange sweet potatoes that grace our Thanksgiving tables under the misnomer "candied yams," we know little about the white-fleshed boniato or the similarly hued Asian varieties that are becoming increasingly available.

Sweet potatoes (the orange ones) are readily available. Purchase firm ones that show no soft spots or blemishes. The boniato and the Asian varieties are available at Caribbean and Asian markets respectively. All are best kept in a cool dark place and should not be refrigerated, as this will change their taste.

Turnips

(Brassica rapa, Rapifera Group)

Related to cabbage, rutabagas, radishes, and mustard, the turnip is a classic northern European vegetable. The root, which is actually the swollen base of the stem, was much prized by the Romans and the Greeks who started them on their culinary conquest of the world.

They're pickled in the Arab world and in parts of Asia, braised, roasted, boiled, and in the sixteenth and seventeenth centuries were even added to salads in Europe. In the southern United States, turnip greens are a delicacy and sometimes they're cooked up with their small turnips still attached.

If you're fortunate enough to find truly tiny purple and white turnips, boil or fry them and then glaze them. In the United States, we usually only get the larger types that require a bit more cooking. Be sure not to overcook turnips; it's one of the culinary crimes that seems to be self-perpetuating. Ten minutes of boiling is usually enough for the small ones.

Select turnips that are heavy and have pearly skins. Be sure that there are no blemishes or soft spots. They'll keep in the refrigerator for only a few days, so purchase just as much as you need.

Three-Root Gratin *Serves 6 to 8*

Winter is the time par excellence to indulge in a love of root vegetables. Few dishes show off the varieties and complexities of their taste like a gratin. This one combines the creamy blandness of potatoes with the freshness of celery root and the sweetness of parsnips. There's even a fourth root vegetable in the zing of the horseradish.

Unsalted butter for greasing the pan
1½ pounds (about 4 large) Yukon Gold potatoes
1½ pounds (1 medium) celery root
½ pound (2 to 3 medium) parsnips
1½ cups grated Gruyère cheese,
  plus extra for the topping
2 cloves garlic, minced
2 tablespoons minced onions
1 tablespoon prepared horseradish, drained
Salt and freshly ground black pepper, to taste
1½ cups chicken stock
Breadcrumbs
2 tablespoons melted unsalted butter

Preheat the oven to 350 degrees and grease a casserole with butter. Wash the potatoes, celery root, and parsnips. Peel them and slice them thinly on a box grater or mandoline. Mix the 1½ cups of cheese, the garlic, onion, and horseradish together. Layer the root vegetables in the casserole first, seasoning each layer with salt and pepper to taste: first a layer of potatoes, followed by one of celery root and one of parsnip, a sprinkle of the cheese mixture, then another of potato and so forth. End with a layer of potato. Pour the chicken stock over the casserole, top with grated cheese and breadcrumbs, and drizzle with the melted butter. Place the dish in the oven and cook uncovered for 1 hour, or until the top is crisp and browned. Serve hot.

Roasted Garlic Mashed Potatoes with Rosemary

Serves 4

Flavored mashed potatoes have become a culinary cliché in recent years. It's gotten so that virtually every restaurant menu has some type of potato flavored with everything from ginger to truffle oil! This is a simple version that adds the creamy richness of roasted garlic to the potatoes, and finishes with a hint of rosemary. The trick is the low-fat yogurt; it makes them much lighter in calories than the usual sour cream. (If you really want to indulge, try the over-the-top Artery Cloggers, p.49.)

2 heads roasted garlic (see page 53)
2 pounds Yukon Gold potatoes, peeled and cut into large dice
1 large onion, coarsely chopped
2 tablespoons unflavored low-fat yogurt, or to taste
Pinch of crushed dried rosemary
Salt and freshly ground black pepper, to taste

The garlic can be roasted beforehand. This can be done while using the oven for another purpose, such as cooking meat, etc., but not while baking!

Place the potatoes and onion in a saucepan, cover with water, and bring to a boil over medium heat. Cover, lower the heat, and simmer for 15 to 20 minutes, or until fork-tender. Drain the potatoes and reserve the liquid. Force the potatoes and onion through a ricer into a bowl. Squeeze the garlic cloves from the papery outside hulls and force them through the ricer. Add the yogurt and just enough of the reserved cooking liquid to the potato mixture to make it creamy smooth. Add the rosemary and salt and pepper, and stir to mix well. Serve hot.

Baked Turnips with Sweet Potatoes, Apples, and Dried Cranberries *Serves 6 to 8*

This recipe was given to me by my friend Alexander Smalls, who loves nothing better than puttering away in the kitchen and coming up with new combinations. In that manner he has written an autobiographical cookbook, *Grace the Table,* and also come up with the inspiration for three wonderful New York City restaurants: Café Beulah, Sweet Ophelia's, and The Shoebox Café. Regrettably, all those have closed, so I truly hope that while he's puttering, he's thinking up a new restaurant concept. (You will too after you taste these turnips.)

2 tablespoons butter, plus extra for the pan

1 pound (about 3) sweet potatoes, peeled and cut into ½-inch dice

2 Granny Smith apples, peeled, cored, and cut into ½-inch dice

2 medium turnips, peeled and cut into ½-inch dice

1 cup dried cranberries

1 tablespoon freshly squeezed lemon juice

3 tablespoons olive oil

Pinch of ground ginger

½ cup packed dark brown sugar

Preheat the oven to 350 degrees. Grease an ovenproof casserole with butter. Place the sweet potatoes, apples, turnips, and cranberries in the casserole, stirring well to mix. Drizzle the lemon juice and oil over the mixture and dot with the 2 tablespoons of butter. Sprinkle with ginger and brown sugar. Place uncovered in the oven and cook for 1½ to 2 hours or until the vegetables are soft. Serve hot.

Mashed Sweet Potatoes with Pineapple *Serves 4 to 6*

Enslaved Africans are probably responsible for the New World confusion between sweet potatoes and yams. When they arrived on this side of the Atlantic, they simply called the tuber that they found by the name of the vegetable they knew. Most of us, unless we are from the Caribbean, Africa, or Asia, have probably never even seen a true yam and almost certainly never cooked one. This recipe will continue the confusion because the growers in Louisiana and Georgia persist in calling their varieties of sweet potatoes yams. Please note the recipe title, though; these are really mashed sweet potatoes.

3 large garnet "yams" (see Note)
2 large carrots, grated
1 cup freshly squeezed orange juice
Pinch of ground ginger
1½ cups minced fresh pineapple

Wash the "yams," peel them, and cut them into 1-inch pieces. Place the "yams" and carrots into a non-reactive saucepan with the orange juice and ginger. Bring to a boil then lower the heat and simmer for 10 to 15 minutes or until the "yams" are fork-tender. Remove them from the liquid, reserving it. Force the mixture through a ricer into a bowl, adding a bit of the cooking liquid if necessary to make a smooth, creamy mix. Add the minced pineapple and stir to mix well. Serve hot.

NOTE: If you read the heading, you all know that these are *not* yams, but that's what they call them at the grocery store, so I'm stuck with it.

Rutabaga Purée   *Serves 6 to 8*

When my family and I used to gather around the Thanksgiving table at my childhood home in Queens, New York, this purée was how I knew that it was Thanksgiving. These rutabagas were made only once a year—on Thanksgiving. As I grew older my kitchen duties ranged from peeling the potato, to cubing the rutabaga, to finally preparing the entire dish. Now that my parents have become ancestors, I have no family of my own, and the man in my life eats no pork, I'm reduced to preparing them for myself, but I still peel and purée at least once a year. . . . After all, it wouldn't be Thanksgiving without them.

> 1 large rutabaga
> 1 medium potato
> 5 strips slab or thick-cut bacon, cut into 1-inch pieces
> Salt and freshly ground black pepper, to taste

Wash the rutabaga and potato, peel them, and cut them into large chunks. Fry the bacon in a heavy saucepan until cooked through but not crisp. Add the vegetables, salt and pepper, and water to cover. Bring to a boil over medium heat; then lower and simmer for 35 minutes, or until the vegetables are fork-tender. Remove the vegetables and bacon, reserving the cooking liquid, and force them through a ricer into a bowl. If necessary, add a bit of the reserved cooking liquid to make a smooth purée. Adjust the seasoning and serve hot.

Guyanese Curried Cabbage and Potatoes *Serves 4 to 6*

If it's in Guyana and it's a vegetable, it will probably end up being curried at one time or another. This is a simple yet delicious way to prepare the winter cabbage instead of the usual brais-ing and boiling. It also brings home a bit of the tropics on a dreary winter day. Let the vegetables cook down a bit so that you can get some of the edges of the cabbage caramelized.

1 tablespooon Madras curry powder

1 teaspoon cider vinegar

1 tablespoon vegetable oil

1 small cabbage (approximately 1 pound), shredded

2 cups peeled, diced Yukon gold potatoes

Prepare a paste with the curry powder and the vinegar. Heat the oil in a heavy skillet and cook the paste over high heat for 1 minute, then add the cabbage and potatoes and cook for an additional minute. Lower the heat, cover, and continue to cook for about 15 minutes or until the cabbage is cooked and the potatoes are fork-tender. (You may need to add some water but the cabbage will release water as it cooks, so don't add too much.) Serve hot with Plain White Rice (see page 54).

SPRING

After the last snowfall, which usually comes some time around my birthday in the middle of March, I begin to have thoughts of spring. Although I wish that my spring fever would take the form of manic housecleaning and organization, it more often manifests itself in the desire for a meal of lamb, asparagus, and new potatoes.

In spring I celebrate the return of life with a return to simplicity. No complicated culinary preparations for me; I celebrate the freshness of the in-coming vegetables with simple sides: steamed, boiled, blanched, and served with the lightest of sauces, if any. It's my way of allowing the taste of the vegetables to shine through.

Spring Favorite Vegetables

Artichokes
(Cynara scolymus)

These members of the thistle family are actually domesticated and cultivated cardoons. No one is quite sure where they originated, but it is thought that they are from the Mediterranean basin, possibly North Africa. They were well-known to the Greeks and the Romans, who associated them with matters sexual; artichokes were thought to be aphrodisiacs. Perhaps this is why they were much loved by the English king, Henry VIII. The word *artichoke* comes from the old Italian *articioco*, which in turn comes from the Arabic word *al-karshuf*, and the vegetable is wildly popular in Italy where small ones are even eaten raw. The larger globe artichokes are more often boiled and eaten with melted butter or a lemony vinaigrette.

Artichokes are readily available year round but the peak season is from March until May. Select artichokes that are compact, heavy, and green. The stalks should be firm. Although artichokes can be kept for several weeks in the refrigerator, they are best when eaten as soon after harvesting as possible, so resist the temptation to stock up.

Asparagus
(Asparagus officinalis)

This member of the lily family grows wild in marshy places throughout Europe, from Poland and the Russian steppes to roadsides in France—virtually anywhere there is well-drained soil. The wild variations are so dispersed that it is somewhat foolhardy to guess an area of origin; some scholars guess that the Mediterranean area is the plant's home.

The name asparagus was used by the Greeks and Romans, and can be traced to the Persian term *asparag,* meaning sprout. For a period of time, the vegetable was known by the poetic term, sparrow grass, an obvious corruption of asparagus.

In Europe, the arrival of the year's first crops of white asparagus inspires a spring worship that is positively pagan in its intensity. Asparagus arrived in the United States with early settlers, but was only grown commercially beginning in the mid-nineteenth century. Here, white asparagus are often forgotten, not really garnering much attention except by those who have had Gallic culinary experiences.

Asparagus is at its peak in the spring. Select firm stalks with tightly furled heads, that are uniform in size to ensure even cooking time. (White asparagus are occasionally available and should be selected in the same manner.) In both cases avoid any yellowish stalks or ones where the ends are mushy. Turn the bunches over and check the bottoms as well as the heads for signs of age. Asparagus doesn't keep well, so purchase only as much as you need and use it rapidly; three days in the refrigerator is about it.

Fiddlehead Ferns
(Matteuccia struthiopteris)

These ellusive vegetables look like tiny green bishop's crooks or the scroll of a violin (hence the name). Not one single plant, but the coiled top of any new fern, fiddleheads mean spring in the

Mid-Atlantic states. In the United States and Canada, the primary type consumed is the baby shoot of the ostrich fern. Fiddleheads were known to the North American Indians long before the arrival of the Europeans, although the ostrich fern seems to have originated in Asia.

Fiddlehead ferns have an astonishingly short period of availability. Their season lasts a scant 15 days. If you're lucky enough to find them fresh at the farmers' market or at your greengrocer, look for ones that are bright forest green, tightly furled, and firm. (They might have some brown, papery scales on them, but that's fine.) They are incredibly perishable and will keep for only a day or so in the refrigerator. The good thing is that they can be blanched, shocked in ice water, and then frozen for future use, but I think that their fragility is what makes them the perfect vegetable for a spring feast.

Peas
(Pisum sativum, Macrocarpon Group)

Peas, also known as green peas, garden peas, or English peas, actually originated in central Asia and Europe. The Chinese first ate them over 4,000 years ago. Charred pea remains have also been found in Neolithic archeological sites in Turkey. These may have been a more mature incarnation of the plant because the green peas that we eat are only immature versions of the same peas that when ripe will become the split peas that turn up in soups. Anyone who remembers high school botany or biology will remember Gregor Mendel's experiments with pea plants, which led to the field of genetics. He was also responsible for cross-breeding peas to produce the first hybridized vegetables.

Dried peas are available all year round. Fresh peas are not always easy to find, but if you're lucky enough to snag some, know that they are best when shelled and cooked soon after picking because the sugar will begin to turn to starch. If you cannot find fresh peas, it's because most of them are frozen or canned, and frozen peas are the best second choice.

Summer Squash
(Cucurbita pepo)

While they are related to cucumbers and melons, squashes are an all-American vegetable. They claim a Central and South American origin, and seeds have been found in burial caves that date back to 8000 B.C. One of the three sister plants that were grown in symbiosis by the native peoples, squashes are grown virtually all over the hemisphere from South America to Canada. Summer squashes, including straightneck, crookneck, zucchini, and pattypan squashes are all picked shortly after flowering when skin and seeds are still edible.

Summer squash in all of its varieties is, as you would expect, at its best in summer, but the season actually begins in the spring. Purchase squash that is solid with shiny skin. Avoid any that are soft or have brown spots. Summer squash does not keep well, so purchase what you need and don't refrigerate it for more than a day or two.

String Beans
(Phaseolus vulgaris)

The string bean (also known as the snap bean, green bean, French bean, wax bean and *haricot vert)* is a member of the New World family of beans that has been a part of the diet of Native Americans for millennia. These New World beans are one of the three sister plants that also include squash and corn. Seeds of cultivated bean plants have been found in Peru that date back to 6000 B.C. The beans were first encountered throughout Latin America by the Spanish explorers and conquistadores in the fifteenth and sixteenth centuries. They and the Portuguese brought them to the rest of the world where the beans were crossed with the European beans of the broad bean family. The resulting mixes have been the bane of botanists' existence ever since. These string beans were originally cultivated from the seeds of the mature beans that are the familiar kidney beans, pinto beans, black beans, flageolets, and others that are eaten fresh or dried; they were only eaten fresh and young beginning in nineteenth-century Italy.

Haricots verts, which are becoming increasingly common, are tiny, intensely flavored pods. Select pods that are uniform in size, crisp, and have no blemishes. They will keep in the refrigerator for up to one week.

Grilled Asparagus with Shaved Parmesan   *Serves 4*

While I usually write about the traditional foods of the African Diaspora, at home I cook dishes from around the world. This Italian classic is one I love to make, especially in the springtime when the first asparagus arrive at the market. Some folks love the thin asparagus that require little preparation; I don't mind the thick, juicy ones that force me to peel the stems. I'm also not afraid to lob off the ends and content myself with the tenderest parts. I've always watched to see whether folks bite off the tips or the ends first; I think it tells a lot about how they like their pleasure. I savor and work my way up to the tips, enjoying each increasingly tasty mouthful. For this recipe you'll need a ridged grill pan and a grater or vegetable peeler.

Oil for the pan
1 pound asparagus
2 tablespoons extra virgin olive oil, or to taste
Parmesan cheese, to taste

Oil a grill pan and heat it. Clean the asparagus, paring the ends if necessary. Place the asparagus on the heated pan and cook for 5 minutes, turning occasionally, so that they are slightly charred in places. Remove and place on a platter. Drizzle the olive oil over the asparagus and shave on as much Parmesan cheese as you dare. (You can also grill the asparagus on a barbecue.)

Artichokes with Lemon Garlic Sauce   *Serves 4*

I learned to eat artichokes in Paris, and find that they make perfect side dishes. I prefer the large globe ones. I've been known to dip them in a ramekin of grainy Dijon mustard, but this sauce is what I make if I'm feeling fancy.

4 large globe artichokes
Cut lemon wedge
3 tablespoons extra virgin olive oil
2 tablespoon freshly squeezed lemon juice
2 teaspoons Dijon mustard
2 cloves garlic, minced, or to taste
Salt and freshly ground pepper, to taste

Remove the outside leaves and snip the thorny tips of the artichokes with kitchen shears. Rub the cut edges with lemon to prevent discoloration. Place the artichokes in water to cover and bring to a boil over high heat. Then lower the heat and simmer for 20 minutes, or until the artichokes are cooked. The artichokes will have darkened and the leaves turned slightly leathery with the soft choke at the bottom. Mix the olive oil, lemon juice, mustard, garlic, and salt and pepper together in a non-reactive bowl and add 1 tablespoon of the cooking water. Place the artichokes in a bowl and drizzle them with the sauce. Serve hot.

NOTE: Eat by peeling the leaves off with your fingers and nibbling off the soft bottom edge. When you reach the center, scrape off the fuzz with a knife, and eat with a knife and fork.

Fiddlehead Ferns   *Serves 4 to 6*

These delicate furled members of various fern species were a surprise to me. I'd eaten them in restaurants and thought preparing them must be a complicated process. When I saw them in the market, I thought I'd try them and was surprised at just how easy they were to fix. Now I pick them up whenever I see them during their brief appearance in spring. (In parts of Canada, they mean summer and don't appear until July.)

1 pound fiddlehead ferns, papery covering brushed off
2 tablespoons butter
6 leaves chives, minced

Trim any ragged edges or hard spots from the stem end of each fern. Bring 2 quarts of water to a boil in a large saucepan. Drop in the ferns and cook for 5 minutes. Drain them and shock them in ice water. Drain again and pat dry with absorbent paper. Heat the butter in a skillet and sauté the ferns for 2 minutes, or until heated through. Serve hot sprinkled with snippets of chives.

Minted Green Peas   *Serves 4*

They're not always easy to find, but nothing quite matches the taste of fresh peas. I even enjoy shelling them. There's something satisfying about the *pop,* the reaming out of each little pod, and the *plop* the peas make as they land in the bowl. A sprig or two of mint added to the cooking water completes this dish that embodies the simplicity of spring.

1½ pounds peas (in the pod)
3 sprigs fresh peppermint
1 tablespoon unsalted butter

Shell the peas and wash the mint. Bring 1 quart of water to a boil in a medium saucepan. Drop in the peas and the mint and cook for 2 to 3 minutes. Drain, place in a serving dish, and top with the butter. Serve piping hot.

Squish (Cooked-down Squash)   *Serves 4*

No, it's not a typographical error: that's what my mother and I called this dish, which she made from zucchini and summer squash. She prepared it in a nonstick saucepan so that if she missed and burned a bit of it, it was easily cleaned out.

3 medium zucchini (green summer squash)
3 medium yellow summer squash

Wash the squash and cut them into ½-inch slices. Place the squash in a nonstick saucepan with ¼ cup of water. Bring to a boil, then lower the heat and cook uncovered for about 5 minutes, or until the liquid is all absorbed and the squash is almost ready to stick. You must watch carefully as this happens really rapidly and the squash can burn. Scrape the squash and brown bits into a serving bowl and serve hot.

Haricots verts à la française

French-style Green Beans   *Serves 4*

This is one of the first recipes that I ever learned to prepare and I still treasure the old French cookbook in which I found it. The tiny baby string beans that are known as *haricots verts* are one of my favorite vegetables. I love to blanch them and sauté them in butter with garlic.

1 pound *haricots verts*
1 tablespoon butter (more if you dare)
1 clove garlic, minced, or to taste
Salt and freshly ground black pepper, to taste

Top and tail the beans. Bring a saucepan of water to a boil add the beans, and cook for 2 to 3 minutes. Drain the beans and shock them in ice water. Drain again and dry them on absorbent paper. Melt the butter in a skillet, add the garlic and the beans and cook, stirring constantly, until the beans are heated through. Season with salt and freshly ground black pepper to taste. Serve hot.

SUMMER

I find early tastes of ripe summer vegetables in New Orleans in June when the Creole tomatoes come into season and the kind gentleman with his selection of heirloom chillies sets up his stand right next to the huge sunflowers. While I savor, select, and delight in the New Orleans bounty, somewhere in my heart I'm really a child of the colder Northeast. Summer somehow always means Martha's Vineyard to me.

Mother Nature pulls out all of the stops with her summer bounty on Martha's Vineyard Island, where I've spent my summers for the past forty-six years. I delight, as I have in decades past, in the fresh tomatoes, remembering the succulent ones from Thimble Farms in the days when my mother and I used to ride out to visit Mrs. Moscow. I always try to pick up a bumper crop of them at the Norton's Farm stand to make into chutney in the last days of August, and have been known to try to make drivers take a detour to get one last batch on the way to the ferry when I head home. Island corn is another delight, with the butter and sugar variety a special summer treat when it arrives in the Reliable supermarket on Oak Bluffs's main street, Circuit Avenue. The twice-weekly farmers' market in Chilmark is a welcome excursion when someone can be snagged to drive me. There, zucchini and their blossoms, all manner of baked and preserved goods, and even fresh fava beans await buyers who stroll through the stalls with their well-behaved Labradors and rambunctious children.

Summer Favorite Vegetables

Bell Peppers
(Capsicum annuum)

One of the earliest plants to be cultivated in Latin America, the bell or sweet pepper is a member of the Solanaceae family that also includes eggplant, tomatoes, and potatoes. As such it is a relative of the hot chilli, with which it is often mixed in salsas. Pepper seeds that date back 5,000 years have been found in Latin America. The Spaniards were responsible for bringing them to Europe where they became mainstays in the Mediterranean region. Sweet or bell peppers can range in color from green to bright reddish orange to deep eggplant black, and are often used to provide color as well as flavor in summer dishes and salsas.

When shopping look for smoothed-skinned peppers with no wrinkles or blemishes. Peppers can be roasted for additional flavor.

Corn
(Zea mays)

Corn, the only native American cereal grain, has been discovered in archeological remains that date back more than 7,000 years. The plant is thought to have originated in Central America and the cosmologies of the Aztecs, Incas, and Maya all include multiple references to corn. It is amply represented in ancient American pottery, jewelry, and art. One of the three sister plants that were grown in harmony, corn was the mother plant for many of the native peoples and is still revered among groups like the Apaches whose shamans use corn pollen as a sacred substance.

While Columbus discovered corn growing in Hispanola on his first voyage, it was Hernán Cortés who brought it to Spain, and the Portuguese who brought it to the world.

Corn should be eaten fresh, as close to the time of picking as possible. The longer it's away from the stalk and the ground, the more the sweetness turns to starch. If fresh corn cannot be found—it really is a summer vegetable—canned or frozen corn kernels may be substituted in some dishes.

Fava Beans
(Vicia faba and Faba vulgaris)

The fava bean or broad bean is an ancient vegetable, thought to have originated in Northern Africa. It was already known to the Chinese more than 5,000 years ago. The Greeks and Romans ate favas as well, and used them not only culinarily but also as ballots in their elections. This is perhaps the origin of the bean or *fève* (bean in French) used to select the king in the traditional King Cake that is served on Epiphany in France, and New Orleans, and wherever francophiles gather.

The beans arrived in the New World shortly after Columbus, crossing the Atlantic westward around the same time that New World varieties arrived in Europe. Before string beans and their New World kin arrived in Europe, fava beans were the only beans known in Europe.

Fava beans are usually found dried in most health food stores and some supermarkets. They are found fresh only for a few months during the late spring and early summer. In season they should be purchased with full plump pods that indicate well-formed beans.

Tomatoes
(Lycopersicon esculentum)

Originally from Mexico and Central America, the tomato has made a long journey to the culinary popularity it holds today. For many years, in fact, tomatoes were considered poison and shunned. Used as an ornamental plant until the eighteenth century, the tomato gradually made its way into the hearts and stomachs of southern Europe and from there to the United States, where it didn't become popular outside of the Creole regions until the nineteenth century. Now it's hard not to find a tomato on any table (particularly when you include ketchup—perhaps the most popular tomato product). Farmers' markets are re-acquainting Americans with the tastes of vine-ripened and heirloom tomatoes, and the love affair is beginning all over again.

Tomatoes are strictly seasonal and should be eaten only in season. Look for them when they are well-colored and firm yet slightly yielding to the touch. If you're going to keep tomatoes in the refrigerator, remove them an hour before serving to allow them to return to room temperature. In the South, gourmets will peel tomatoes before serving them, even in salads. Peel tomatoes by making a cross at the blossom end and plunging them for a few seconds in a saucepan of boiling water; core them and remove the skin with a sharp paring knife (the skin will almost curl away). If you're a real tomato fanatic, buy a serrated tomato knife just for slicing this summer delight.

Ratatouille *Serves 4 to 6*

This is a summer dish I love to prepare. It's a quick version of the classic Mediterranean rata-touille and makes use of all of the wonderful summer vegetables. It's a colorful addition to any summer meal.

4 tablespoons olive oil

1 large onion, sliced

1 medium green bell pepper, cored and diced

1 medium yellow bell pepper, cored and diced

1 medium eggplant, stemmed and diced

2 medium zucchini, cut into 1-inch chunks

5 medium ripe tomatoes, peeled, seeded, and cut into wedges

1 tablespoon minced flat-leaf parsley

⅛ teaspoon dried oregano

1 teaspoon dried basil

2 large garlic cloves, minced

Salt and freshly ground black pepper, to taste

Heat the oil in a large skillet, add the onion, and sauté until it is translucent, about 3 minutes. Add the bell peppers and eggplant and continue to cook for five minutes, stirring occasionally. Add the zucchini and tomatoes, lower the heat, and simmer, covered, for 20 minutes or until they are cooked through. Add the parsley, oregano, basil, garlic, and salt and pepper and continue to cook for an additional 10 minutes. The dish may be served hot, chilled, or at room temperature.

Corn Fritters with Shrimp   *Serves 4*

This is a variation on a Southeast Asian dish, and can be served as an appetizer, a snack, or a side dish. Whichever way, these fritters are sure to disappear. You may add more shrimp, or leave them out entirely.

Vegetable oil for frying
6 ears sweet summer-fresh corn
3 medium shrimp, peeled and minced
4 shallots, peeled and minced
2 cloves garlic, minced
1 small red chilli, or to taste, stemmed and minced
1 teaspoon ground coriander seed
1 egg, beaten
Salt and freshly ground black pepper, to taste

Heat the oil to 375 degrees in a deep, heavy saucepan or Dutch oven. Cut the corn kernels off the cobs and place into a medium bowl. Add the shrimp, shallots, garlic, chilli, coriander, egg, salt and pepper, and mix well.

Drop the mixture into the oil 1 tablespoon at a time and fry for 2½ minutes on each side, or until the fritters are golden brown. (Be careful not to crowd them as it will slow down cooking time.) Drain on absorbent paper and serve hot or at room temperature.

Okra, Corn, and Tomatoes   *Serves 4 to 6*

This dish is one that can be prepared year-round as the ingredients stand up well to canning or freezing. But when I serve this dish in the dead of winter on my New Year's table, I know that the taste is never as bright as it is mid-summer when it's prepared with the freshest ingredients.

½ pound fresh young okra pods, topped
2 cups corn kernels cut off the cob (about 6 ears)
4 large summer-ripe tomatoes, peeled, seeded, and coarsely chopped
1 habanero chilli, pricked with a fork
Salt and freshly ground black pepper, to taste

Select the smallest okra pods that you can find. If the pods are longer than 3 inches, cut them into ½-inch slices. Place the okra, corn, tomatoes, and chilli in a medium saucepan. Season with salt and pepper. Bring to a boil over high heat, then lower the heat, cover, and cook for 15 minutes or until the flavors have blended. Remove and discard the chilli when the dish has reached the desired degree of spiciness. Serve hot.

Zucchini Flower Fritters   *Serves 4*

Zucchini flowers are not easy to find unless you grow your own zucchini and have a bumper crop. If that's the case, you might want to try this recipe for the flowers of the summer squash stuffed with a mixture of rice, chèvre cheese, and seasonings.

1 cup cooked rice (see page 54)
3 tablespoons chèvre cheese
2 tablespoons minced flat-leaf parsley
1 tablespoon minced chives
Salt and freshly ground black pepper, to taste
8 unsprayed zucchini flowers, rinsed and patted dry
¼ cup all-purpose flour
¼ cup ice water
Hot sauce, to taste
Vegetable oil for deep frying

Prepare the stuffing by mixing together the rice, chèvre, parsley, chives, and salt and pepper. Gently fill each blossom with the stuffing, tucking the petals in to cover the filling. Place the flour in a small bowl and drizzle in just enough water to make a thin, runny batter. Season the batter with salt and hot sauce. Heat the oil for frying to 375 degrees in a deep, heavy saucepan or Dutch oven. Dip the blossoms into the batter and gently place them in the oil. Fry for 3 minutes, or until golden brown, then remove and drain on absorbent paper. Serve hot.

Corn on the Cob with Herbed *Pimentón* Butter

Serves 4 to 6

Corn is a leitmotif in my summer menus. When it's fresh and sweet, I just can't get enough of it. While I like it in fritters and succotashes, my favorite way is simply boiled for a few minutes and then slathered with whatever herbed butter is my favorite of the moment. This was last summer's favorite, a lime–*pimentón*–herb butter.

3 tablespoons salted butter
2 teaspoons olive oil
¼ teaspoon freshly grated lime zest
1 teaspoon freshly squeezed lime juice
½ teaspoon minced fresh basil leaves
⅛ teaspoon hot *pimentón,* or to taste (see Note)
8 to 12 ears of corn, shucked and silk removed

Prepare the butter by mixing the butter, oil, lime zest and juice, basil, and *pimentón* together in a small bowl. Cover with plastic wrap and refrigerate for 2 hours. When you're ready to serve, bring a stockpot full of water to a rolling boil. Add the ears of corn, cover, lower the heat to simmer, and cook for 5 to 7 minutes, or until the corn is tender. Drain and serve piping hot with the butter on the side for slathering.

NOTE: *Pimentón* is a Spanish spice, also known as smoked paprika. It is made by grinding smoke-dried peppers.

Year-Round Favorites

Some vegetables have become year-round staples, ignoring the rules of seasonality. They're always available and always delicious.

Broccoli
(Brassica oleraca var. italica)

Broccoli is a member of the cabbage family. It is botanically so close to cauliflower as to be indistinguishable. Like cauliflower, a tight cluster of plant buds make up the head and some scholars feel it is a cauliflower ancestor. The name broccoli comes from the Italian word meaning little arms or little shoots. An ancestor of Albert (Cubby) Broccoli, the late James Bond movie producer, is reputed to have been one of the popularizers of the vegetable when it arrived in North America in the eighteenth century.

Broccoli should be evenly colored and have firm branches with compact clusters of florets. It's readily available year-round, but perishable, so purchase only what you need—it doesn't keep well for more than 5 or 6 days.

Carrots
(Daucus carota, Sativus Group)

The Moors are to blame or praise for the introduction of the carrot into the diet of Europe. The original carrots were almost purple in color, tough, and woody. They did not gain popularity until the Renaissance and were not transformed into the orange roots we know today until the mid-nineteenth century. By 1879, author and gastronome Alexandre Dumas would attest to the fact that to his taste the pale yellow or white carrots were the best. In India, carrots are often almost red in color, a startling culinary surprise. They prove though to be as sweet as the more familiar orange ones.

Carrots are readily available and store well. When eaten raw, as they are in some *sambals*, they are an excellent source of vitamin A and potassium. Select firm carrots that have no damp or discolored spots.

Garlic
(Allium sativum)

The big stinker of the onion family, garlic has been cultivated for over 5,000 years, making it one of the world's oldest cultivated plants. Heads of the plant have been found in Egyptian tombs, and it was given to the slaves who built the pyramids with the thought that its strong fragrance would give strength to the workers. Athletes in ancient Greece consumed it for its alleged strength-giving properties as well. A section of the Athenian market was known simply as *ta skorda,* the garlic.

With the popularity of the stinking lily, there was also some concern about its odor. It was consumed mainly by the working classes, so it was considered vulgar to smell of it. Horace wrote that garlic was more harmful than hemlock in that it could make a lover refuse a kiss or retreat to the far side of the bed. It still can, so most folks eat it *à deux.* Roasted, the cloves take on a nutty sweetness as the pungency mellows out; this way garlic can delight even the most finicky eater and leave no aftereffect. The plant was also alleged to have magical powers and as we all know, it will keep vampires away as well as lovers.

Garlic is readily available so there is no excuse for using garlic salt or garlic powder. Look for plump, firm heads of garlic that are free from blemishes. If you use a lot of garlic, as I do, you may even want to break down and keep a string of it in the kitchen where it will be decorative as well as useful.

Mushrooms

The term *mushroom* has been used to cover a wide variety of edible fungi ranging from puffballs to truffles. *Champignons de Paris,* often called common mushrooms, get their name because they were cultivated in abandoned rock quarries in the Parisian area; they are readily available. Cremini or crimini mushrooms, also sold as "Baby Bellas," Roman, or Golden Italians, are no more than young portobello mushrooms. They and their more mature relatives are also found just about everywhere.

When shopping, remember that small mushrooms with closed caps and no visible gills are best for cooking whole. Large closed ones are good for slicing, and those with caps flared and gills visible are the most flavorful. They'll last for about a week or so in the refrigerator and will keep better in a paper bag than in plastic, which will soften and rot them. You don't have to peel mushrooms; just rinse them lightly, blot dry and, if necessary, clean them with a very soft brush—special mushroom brushes are sold, but a baby toothbrush will do just fine.

Artery Cloggers *Serves 4*

These over-the-top, full-of-everything mashed potatoes are my way of having it all. I certainly wouldn't dare eat them too often, but they're worth waiting for. I first came up with the idea when I was the resident food historian on Sara Moulton's *Cooking Live Primtime* show on the Food Network. They're truly delicious.

6 medium Yukon Gold potatoes, peeled and quartered
½ teaspoon salt
4 tablespoons unsalted butter, at room temperature
4 to 5 tablespoons heavy cream, heated
1 head roasted garlic (page 53), squeezed into a ramekin
2 tablespoons freshly made bacon bits (chopped cooked bacon)
Salt and freshly ground black pepper, to taste

Place the potatoes in 4 cups of water in a heavy saucepan and cook, covered, for 15 to 20 minutes. When the potatoes are soft, drain them and put through a food mill. Add the salt, butter, cream, garlic, and bacon. Season to taste and stir to make sure all of the ingredients are thoroughly mixed. Serve immediately. Yum!

Ful Medames

Egyptian Fava Beans *Serves 4 to 6*

This Egyptian dish is a year-round treat, as it is prepared with dried fava beans, not the fresh ones that are only available in early summer where I live. It's fun to let your guests serve themselves and then add the garnishes as they like. In that way *ful* becomes a side with sides. However, it's often the entire meal in Egypt.

2 cups dried broad beans or Italian fava beans
6 cloves garlic, or to taste
1 teaspoon sea salt, or to taste
1 tablespoon freshly squeezed lemon juice
¼ cup olive oil
1½ teaspoons minced flat-leaf parsley

Garnishes
1 dozen small radishes
3 hard-boiled eggs, quartered
6 small scallions, cleaned and trimmed
1 package pita bread, cut into wedges
  and toasted

Wash the beans and pick them over, removing any debris and discolored ones. Place the beans in a large stockpot with 4 cups of water and allow them to soak overnight. The next day add water to cover and bring to a boil over medium heat. Lower the heat and simmer for 2 hours, or until very tender. (You may need to add more water. If so, add only boiling water or the beans will toughen.)

While the beans are cooking, mash the garlic and the sea salt together in a food processor. Gradually add the lemon juice, oil, and parsley, pulsing until you have a thick liquid. When the beans are soft, drain them, reserving some of the cooking liquid. Add the garlic mixture and 1 tablespoon of the cooking liquid to the beans and stir well. Serve the beans in a deep platter surrounded by the garnishes. Each diner takes a serving of beans and the garnishes of choice.

Carrots with Orange Juice and Ginger   *Serves 4*

With cooking, as in other areas of life, necessity is always the mother of invention. I remember one day in my early kitchen years I ran out of pearl onions while preparing a coq au vin and substituted black-eyed peas for a dish that while certainly not classically French, was tasty and appealing. These carrots were a less controversial accident and are now a part of my ready-at-any-time repertoire. You can even drain the cooking liquid, chill it, and drink it later.

6 medium carrots, peeled and sliced into ½-inch slices
1½ cups freshly squeezed orange juice
1 thumb-sized piece of ginger, peeled and minced
Salt and freshly ground black pepper, to taste

Place the carrots, orange juice, and ginger in a medium, non-reactive saucepan and season with salt and pepper. Bring to a boil over high heat. Lower the heat to a simmer and cook for 10 minutes, or until the carrots are fork-tender. Drain and serve hot.

NOTE: This can also be cooked in the microwave for 3 to 5 minutes, stirring occasionally, depending on the microwave power level.

Champignons a l'ail

Mushrooms with garlic   *Serves 4 to 6*

This is another French favorite I first encountered when I spent my junior year of college in Paris. There, the father of the family with whom I lived would do the marketing each Sunday, and return with the freshest mushrooms, which he would sauté with butter and garlic. For someone who came from a garlic-free household where mushrooms were never on the menu, the dish was a revelation. These mushrooms are perfect with steaks; I'm not a gravy person, but I rarely prepare a steak or hamburger without having a small dish of these mushrooms on the side.

1 (10-ounce) box of cremini mushrooms
1 tablespoon unsalted butter
1 tablespoon olive oil
4 cloves garlic, minced, or to taste
Salt and freshly ground black pepper, to taste

Clean and slice the mushrooms. Heat the butter and oil in a skillet until the butter foams. Add the garlic and the mushrooms and sauté for five minutes, or until the mushrooms are browned. Season with salt and freshly ground black pepper to taste. Serve hot.

Roasted Garlic   *Serves 1*

It's hooray for the stinking lily with this garlic recipe that I use whenever I make any kind of roasted meat. I shove a few heads in the roasting pan so that I've got some in the refrigerator to use if I want to just slather a clove or two on some bread. The garlic completely loses its bite and becomes unctuous, aromatic, and irresistible.

1 head of garlic
Oil for the baking dish

Slice off the top of the head of garlic so that the tips of each clove show. Remove the papery outer layers and place the head cut side down in a greased baking dish filled with 1 inch of water. (If you're cooking the garlic with a roast, the pan drippings take the place of water.) Bake at 450 degrees for 1 hour, or until the cloves soften. When done, remove the garlic from the oven and serve warm with toasted crusty bread, or use whenever roasted garlic is called for.

Plain White Rice   *Serves 4 to 6*

It's time for a culinary confession: I used to make the world's worst rice. I resorted to Minute Rice, boil-in-the-bag rice, and just about every other thing I could try to get it right, but it just didn't work. I could never cook rice. My mother was always assigned the task when we ate together and I, who am not overly fond of potatoes, had been missing her hand at the rice pot since her death.

Then, as I was cooking for my friend Oumar who harks from Senegal where rice-eating is a way of life, I heard my mother's voice in my head saying, "Cook rice like you cook pasta." Bingo! I stopped measuring and now get it right every time. The trick is to cook the rice in a big pot of boiling water until it is al dente, drain it, then steam it in a colander until finished.

1 cup long grain white rice
Butter, salt, and freshly ground black pepper, to taste

Fill a 5-quart saucepan with water and bring it to a boil over high heat. Add the rice, cover, and lower the heat to a simmer. Cook for 15 minutes, or until the rice is al dente. Drain the rice and place it in a colander over the same pot filled with 2 to 4 inches of water that you slowly bring to a boil. Once the water reaches a boil, continue for 2 minutes more. Fluff the rice with a fork, place it in a serving bowl, season with butter, salt, and pepper and serve hot.

Chapter 2

SALADS AND SLAWS

Somehow, I don't remember savoring the salads of my youth. They fade into a pale blur the shade of iceberg lettuce. There was my mother's potato salad, pristine pure: potatoes, celery, onions, and, if she was feeling frisky, a mince of green bell pepper. There was her cole slaw: shreds of cabbage with a mayonnaise-y dressing, and occasionally a mix of carrots and dark, plump raisins. Winters brought a ruby red beet salad of (dare I say it) canned beets mixed with mild onion and topped with a sweet-and-sour vinaigrette. Summers were a slurry of cooling thin cucumber slices dressed with the same sweetened cider vinegar.

My salad epiphany would occur years later in Paris, home to so many culinary "Ah-ha's." There, in a restaurant called Chez Garin on the Left Bank, I truly understood what a salad could mean to a meal. I had been dazzled by the meal prepared by Georges Garin, the chef whose restaurant was the favorite haunt of André Malraux and others. I had been astonished by my meal: a dense velvety slab of *pâté de foie gras,* a truffle stew, a saddle of lamb, perfectly rosy pink, with a crust of crisp bread-crumbs and spices. The accompanying *haricots verts* have defined all subsequent green beans for me. Then, in a pause before the cheese course, it arrived: a bowl in which a whiff of garlic mixed with the fragrance of lamb to flavor a handful of crisp, buttery, light green leaves, topped with a dressing that mastered the principle of just enough red wine vinegar, olive and walnut oils, and a hint of mustard. The salad was heightened with a sprinkling of salt to bring all of the tastes into sharp focus. The classic *salade verte* tied up all of the flavors of the main course and left my mouth ready to proceed to the meal's end, refreshed. The simplicity and the perfection of each ingredient was startling even to one who was used to eating well (my mother was no slouch in the kitchen department!).

Since that day over thirty years ago, salads have become my passion. While many Americans abroad miss hamburgers and fries, I frequently find myself craving a simple salad with the yearning of an emigrant dreaming of home. I have learned that salads exist around the world; the trick is to identify them in their many different places on the menu, and, when given the opportunity, to select and savor.

My parents had an apartment in the South of Spain for a brief time. There I learned that while a Spanish *ensalada mixta* could be had at virtually any café, my favorite salad in southern Spain— and arguably the most refreshing one—is the one that comes to the table in a small bowl and is called gazpacho. The mix of tomato, garlic, onion, and stale bread produces a fragrant cooling broth that is given density by the addition of finely minced bits of onion, cucumber, tomato, bell pepper, and buttery croutons at the last minute according to the diner's preference. There's even a white version prepared from pounded almonds and garlic, garnished with green grapes.

In Morocco I learned that salads—*salades*—come first—and sometimes again last, as they do in Tunisia and Egypt. They are a raft of savory small plates that may be marinated fava beans or cooked carrot pieces topped with a vinaigrette and snippets of cilantro. There may be roasted peppers drizzled with a fragrant oil, or a mash of zucchini, or a plate of beet cubes topped with a slick of olive oil. Meals, from the simplest daily lunch to the most elaborate *diffa,* or banquet, all begin with this opening salvo that changes with the seasonal availability of ingredients.

Further down the African continent, salads are a modern addition to the diet and appear only on westernized tables, if at all. Their recent adoption in no way impedes the cooks' inventiveness. Before the country's current strife, the seasonal arrival in the market of buttery avocados of the Côte d'Ivoire was an incentive for local chefs to get busy in the kitchen. The avocados were accompanied by everything from shrimp and crabmeat to chunks of the sweet, ripe pineapples that always seemed to arrive at the same time. Before the arrival of tourism in West Africa placed salads on hotel menus, canny colonials improvised the salads they knew from local ingredients in Ghana, Nigeria, Côte d'Ivoire, and elsewhere. They used native yams instead of potatoes to produce yam salads, and dressed colorful arrangements of canned vegetables. Further south in South Africa, the Islamic culinary aesthetic prevails in the cooking of the Cape Malay and small plates again accompany the meal. The Swahili coast culture of eastern Africa that prevails along the Indian Ocean from Kenya to Tanzania melds the small plates of the Islamic world with the culinary traditions of the East, and savory nibbles of pickles may appear on the table at any point in the meal.

I've also savored salads in the East. The one trip I took to India the year my father died left me with a lasting desire to return to the subcontinent and a love of the minced salad known as *katchumber* and the savory mix of vegetables and yogurt known as *raita.* Cooling and refreshing, they are the perfect accompaniment to the spicier dishes.

Farther east, dishes like the bonito flake-topped, soy-flavored cooked spinach known as *oshitashi* and the sweet density of *hijiki* could pass as salads on any western menu, and the hybrid soy, sesame, and rice wine vinegar dressing that adorns the iceberg in many a stateside Japanese eatery has become one of the most ubiquitous examples of East meets West fusion.

Aside from the African-American classics that imprinted their tastes on my soul during my 1950s childhood when they were offered by my mother, the New World offers its own array of salads. In the north, the Caesar is a must even in these days when the traditional coddled egg may not be the wisest thing for health reasons. The thick summery tomatoes of Martha's Vineyard and New Jersey, the juicy firm Creoles of New Orleans, or even the Ugly-Ripes from an Atlanta supermarket just seem to cry out for a drizzle of olive oil and a hint of basil or, as my grandmother would add, a pinch of sugar to bring out their sweetness.

The cassava that Columbus was served on his first meeting with a Caribbean *cacique* turns up cooked and dressed in a garlicky sauce on some Cuban tables. The French islands grate the vegetable squash known as mirliton in New Orleans, *chocho* in Jamaica, *xuxu* in Brazil, and *chayote* in the Hispanic world and in much of the U.S. It's then mixed with a vinaigrette and served over lettuce. Sweet potatoes, either the orange variety or the classic *boniato,* come to the table dressed for dinner as do all manner of vegetables from asparagus to zucchini. In Brazil, they even blanch okra and serve it with lettuce in a savory sauce. The cucumber salad that I so loved as a child arrives with an extra zip in Jamaica, where the heat of minced Scotch Bonnet peppers is added to its cane vinegar and oil dressing.

Back in the United States where I began my culinary journey I am gob-smacked daily by the array of ingredients that now turn up as salads. First spinach came out of the bag and then there were romaine, and arugula with its large spicy leaves. Some of my recent discoveries include spicy greens like Asian *mizuna* and tiny leaves of the same mustard greens that my paternal grandmother used to serve stewed down as a meal. There's radicchio and Lolla Rossa, endive and Bibb, Boston and baby spinach and borage. Mixtures of fresh herbs include everything from parsley to dill to fennel, of which every part is used, from the bulb to the feathery leaves. Even the iceberg lettuce that has been so reviled is making a comeback and I now find myself keeping a head in the refrigerator for those days when I want the comforting watery crunch topped with a crumble of blue cheese—one of my favorite childhood memories.

The Making of a Salad

In 1699, John Evelyn penned a treatise on the importance of salads entitled *Acetaria: A Discourse on Sallets*. In it he states:

> . . . in the composure of a sallet, every plant should come in to bear its part, without being overpower'd by some herb of stronger taste, so as to endanger the native sapor and vertue of the rest; but fall into their places, like the notes in music, in which there should be nothing harsh or grating: and tho' admitting some discords (to distinguish and illustrate the rest) striking in the more sprightly, and sometimes gentler notes, reconcile all dissonances, and melt them into an agreeable composition.

Evelyn's comparison of a salad to music is apt in that balance is required in both. He further enjoins readers that "lettuces, cresses, radishes, &c. (as was directed) must be exquisitely pick'd, clean'd, wash'd, and put into the strainer; swing'd and shaken gently." Evelyn is again right on the money, for no matter how exotic or expensive the ingredients, nothing can ruin the taste of a salad more than a mouthful of grit or a slimy rotted leaf.

Give salads the honor they have merited for over three centuries with a few basic tools. A salad spinner will wash and dry the picked-over leaves. If you don't own one, the spinner can be replaced with a colander or a sieve and some absorbent paper. Buy leaves in small quantities and keep them fresh in the refrigerator by removing them from the plastic bags they may come in, washing them, and wrapping them in a damp tea towel for a day or so until use. Whole heads of lettuce should be kept in the crisper drawer of the refrigerator.

While not crucial, a salad bowl is a delight. Remember that glass or porcelain are best; no metal bowls of any sort no matter how beautiful or fancy, as the metal can react with the vinegar in the dressing. Wood, while decorative, will hold the odors and flavors of the oil and the garlic and over time may become disagreeable. If you're an antique tableware junkie, as I am, you might even want to try to find some of the old crescent-shaped bone china plates that hug the main plate and make perfect dishes for side salads.

Serve It Forth

A final note: while we in the United States tend to begin our meal with a salad or nibble away at it throughout the meal, don't be afraid to use the salad as a grace note at the end of the meal in the European manner, to tie together some of the flavors. Rub a bruised garlic clove around the bowl before adding the leaves. Add perhaps a whisper of pan drippings from a roast for a *je ne sais quoi* hint of taste. Keep an array of oils and vinegars in your pantry and purchase them in small sizes so that they retain their freshness. In Elizabethan England, cooks used all sorts of ingredients in their salads—from violet buds to sage leaves and occasionally fruit. I use fruit as well as flowers to add interest to my salads. A handful of blueberries or raspberries nestled among the green leaves in the fall, a few tablespoonfuls of pomegranate seeds perk up things in the winter, and a few bright nasturtiums add their peppery flavor to a summer mix. In a nod to the potato salad I once tasted in a favorite Korean restaurant, I may add a few peeled bits of Granny Smith apple to bring brightness and crunch. The trick with any salad or slaw is to select the freshest ingredients, clean them scrupulously, dress them appropriately to their composition (don't douse light leaves with mayonnaise!), and serve them forth with love.

Salad Bowl Basics

Today, just about everything that can turn up on the plate is fair game for the salad bowl. However, there are still basic building blocks of a classic salad: lettuce, oil, vinegar, and salt and pepper.

Salad Greens

There are three basic types of salad greens: lettuce leaves, other leaves, and members of the *brassica* or cabbage family.

Lettuce leaves

Lettuce is a native of the eastern Mediterranean and its cultivation can be traced back as far as 4500 B.C. The English word comes from the Latin *lactus* meaning milk; it is thought that the plants were named for the milky sap that exudes from the stems when the heads are cut. The Greeks and Romans used lettuce not only as a vegetable, but also as a remedy. Columbus is thought to have brought lettuce to the New World. There are over 100 varieties of lettuces grown today, ranging from iceberg to celtuce, a cross between lettuce and celery.

There are three types of lettuces. There are head lettuces, with round hearts and loose or tight leaves. Typical examples include Boston lettuce, smaller-leaved Bibb lettuce, and the much-maligned iceberg. Long-leaf lettuces are made up of variants of the lettuce we call romaine in the U.S., but that is known as Cos elsewhere for the Greek island where the Romans are reputed to have discovered it. Finally, loose-leaf lettuce, the largest of the three groups, includes all of the lettuces that do not have an obvious head, such as the red leaf and green leaf lettuces that are readily available in supermarkets and greengrocers.

Other leaves

This group includes members of the chicory and endive families as well as other edible leaves. Chicory is thought to have originated in the Mediterranean basin. The classic French salad *frisée aux lardons,* chicory with bacon, uses the curly leaves to good advantage. Escarole, which has wider leaves, is also a member of this family, as is radicchio, a plant that originated in northern Italy where it has been in recorded use since the sixteenth century. The confusion sets in as some folks refer to the curly-leafed chicory as endive. It is compounded by the fact that in England, the slim, firm-headed whitish-yellow lettuce that we know in America as endive or Belgian endive is known as witloof chicory or Belgian chicory.

Arugula is a peppery leaf that was known to the Romans. It's sometimes called Italian cress, rocket, or even *roquette* in French and in some old recipes from New Orleans.

Dandelion greens (the common garden pest) are as most gardeners know, a hardy perennial thought to be native to Europe, northern Africa, central and northern Asia, and North America. The English name of the plant comes from the French *dent de lion* meaning "lion's tooth" and referring to the jagged edges of the leaves. The other French name—*pissenlit* or "wet the bed"—refers to the plant's diuretic properties. While dandelions grow almost everywhere, foragers should be careful to avoid picking those along the sides of the roads, as they have been tainted by pollution. Also, the leaves are best when picked young. Dandelion greens are becoming more widely available in supermarkets, good news for those who don't have the urge to clear up their neighbor's garden.

Mache, also known as lamb's lettuce or corn salad, is an annual plant closely related to catnip and valerian. The small, deep green, velvety leaves go well with milder lettuces.

Watercress is mentioned in Greek writing dating from the first century A.D. The smooth, round leaves add a peppery note to any salad. The plant was known to the Greeks and the Romans as nasturtium, from the Latin word for twisted nose, an indication of the face folks pulled after eating the bitey plant. The nasturtium that we know today is also edible, from its orange, yellow, or red flowers to its peppery leaves and seeds. This plant, though, is of South American origin and was originally called Indian cress. If using nasturtium or any other edible flowering plant in a salad, make sure that it has been grown for human consumption. Watercress is available in most supermarkets.

Spinach may be a native of Persia. It is thought to have been brought to Spain by the Moors and spread from there to the rest of Europe. Florentine Catherine de Medici brought spinach with her when she arrived in France in 1533 to marry King Henry II. In her honor, classical French cooking refers to all dishes served on a bed of spinach as *à la Florentine*. When buying spinach at the supermarket, forget the bag and instead look for fresh bunches of leaves. If you're preparing a spinach dish, wash, wash, and then wash again; nothing's worse then a mouth full of grit.

Members of the *brassica* family

Members of the cabbage or *brassica* family which turn up in the salad bowl include green cabbage, white cabbage, and red cabbage, as well as Savoy cabbage and some of the Chinese cabbages such as celery cabbage *(pe-tsai)*. These greens usually show up in slaws, but if blanched and shredded may find their way into winter salads. I like to use the milder red cabbage for color instead of bitter radicchio.

Mustard is also a member of the *brassica* family and the plant—from leaves to seeds—seems to have been eaten in the Mediterranean region since antiquity. (Mustard the condiment is prepared from the seeds of the plant, which exists in about 40 varieties, and is discussed in Chapter 5.) The mature leaves are cooked mainstays in many an African-American kitchen in the United States, and the young and tender leaves add wonderfully peppery notes to any salad.

The Japanese green *mizuna* is a new addition to my salad bowl. The plant is of Chinese origin and has been cultivated in Japan for centuries. The green leaves look a bit like dandelion greens, but pack a hot wallop in the mouth. Tiny tender leaves add a more delicate heat, and turn up in the Asian salad mixes or spicy salad mixes found at farmers' markets and better greengrocers.

A note about mesclun

The term *mesclun* has been so bandied about that most of us have forgotten, if we ever knew, that it originated in Provence, France. There, it refers to a mix of small tender baby greens. The traditional mix may include young leaves of arugula, dandelion, parsley, watercress, and other edible greens. Mesclun mixes are widely available at grocery stores.

Oils

In my nuclear-family, suburban upbringing in the 1950s, olive oil was an exotic ingredient that rarely made an appearance. My childhood salads were topped with a homemade dressing prepared with (dare I say it) regular vegetable oil, cider vinegar, a dash of mustard and ketchup, and a pinch of sugar. In later years, even the Four Seasons packages that came attached to the nifty salad dressing mixer bottle did not specify what type of oil. How things have changed. Today my pantry fairly bursts with oils in different varieties and tastes, and I marvel at just how far we've come.

Olive oil

The one small bottle of olive oil in my mother's pantry has exploded into a veritable industry that requires a shelf all its own at even the most modest of specialty shops.

Olive oil is the oil of a generation; we add it as a nostrum to our daily diet, swear by its healthful properties, and delight in telling ourselves that this is a good fat that will prolong our lives as well as give us great tasting food.

I'm not exactly sure where I fit in the nutrition wars, but I do know that olive oil offers a range of flavors no other oil matches and that's enough for me. I usually have two or three different bottles of it on my pantry shelves. There's a supermarket brand like Bertolli for frying and general use where the taste is not of primary importance. An aromatic bottle of extra virgin is there for use in salad dressings and when I feel like making homemade mayonnaise or other dishes where I want the flavor of the oil to shine through. Finally, there's a bottle of specialty oil I keep in reserve; it ensures that I never run out.

Deborah Krasner's *The Flavors of Olive Oil: A Tasting Guide and Cookbook* is a small tome that will rapidly become a bible for further olive oil study. She demystifies the difference between extra virgin olive oils and others, informing readers that extra virgin olive oils are so labeled because by regulation they must have less than 1 percent acidity, be mechanically (not chemically) produced, and usually are the result of oil extraction taking place within twenty-four hours of harvesting or less. She reminds us that olives are grown in more than thirty-five countries around the globe, and many countries produce several varieties of olive oil. Those interested in going into greater depth with olive oils will find that her hints for tastings and her classification of the olive oils according to four basic flavor types—delicate, fruity, olive-y, and leafy—will clear up any confusion. The secret with olive oil, as with any other culinary ingredient, is in your mouth. Taste, taste, taste; the differences among the olive oils are startling and in some cases so flagrant you'll wonder why you hadn't noticed them before.

Remember that olive oil, like any other oil, has a limited life and will oxidize. Purchase it from shops where there is a good turnover and a wide variety. Store it in a cool dark place and use it often.

Other oils

While olive oil in all of its seemingly infinite variety is the major salad oil of choice for most, new types of oil are being added to the national pantry daily. For a change, try adding a bit of walnut or hazelnut oil to the dressing. These oils have been used for years in France and add that inexplicable something to French salad dressings.

I also like to add a dash or two of roasted sesame oil to my vinaigrette for the dark, nutty taste it brings. I even add a bit to the Japanese dressing of soy sauce and rice wine vinegar with a pinch of sugar that is a fusion classic.

There are safflower oils, corn oils, sunflower seed oils, peanut oils, and even the plain old generic vegetable oil of my youth, although I suspect few would even consider using it in a salad today.

Herb-infused oils can be purchased or created at home by adding about one-quarter cup of chopped fresh herbs to two cups of oil, tightly closing the bottle, and allowing the flavors to infuse for two weeks. The oil is then strained and decanted into a jar. A few sprigs of the herb can be added and the jar is tightly sealed and ready to use.

Vinegars

Balsamic vinegar

If olive oil is the queen of oils, balsamic vinegar is the emperor of vinegars. True balsamic vinegar is a far cry from the diluted liquid found on most supermarket shelves. True *aceto balsamico tradizionale* has a honey-like consistency, with a haunting, almost wine-y flavor. A small phial of it is extremely expensive but worth every penny, and it's doled out in eye dropper-size portions. It is traditionally used as a condiment or an *adorno* to finish a dish of roasted asparagus topped with shavings of Parmesan cheese, or to stir into a soup or drizzle on a mayonnaise-topped carpaccio. The rich, dark flavors of traditional balsamic, which can cost more than $500 for a scant three ounces, are the result of years of aging. A saying in Modena, home of balsamic vinegar, insists that the person who begins the process will not taste the vinegar; rather his sons and grandsons will taste it. This is true, despite the patriarchal rhetoric. The process takes at least twelve but may take as many as forty or more years. The grapes are picked at their ripest, crushed, and pressed into a juice called *mosto* or must, which is then cooked for twenty-four to thirty hours until it becomes a sweet concentrate of flavors. The cooked must is then placed into the largest of a series of wooden barrels, each made of a different wood, called a *batteria* and allowed to ferment. Over the twelve years required by law for the preparation of *aceto balsamico tradizionale,* as the vinegar is transferred from barrel to barrel, the water evaporates and the remaining vinegar becomes a dark, rich concentrate of flavors. The $4.99 bottles on the shelf, or for that matter even the $25 ones, are pale versions of the original. Most of us cannot afford a real bottle of balsamic vinegar and if we can, we certainly don't use it for salad dressing. So we content ourselves with whatever price point and taste point makes us happiest. My rule of thumb about balsamic is that if the recipe calls for more than a scant drizzle, I know that the author really means I should use my favorite example of whatever version I can afford. I proceed accordingly and so should you.

Other vinegars

The word vinegar comes from the French *vin aigre* or "sour wine" and most are produced by the acid fermentation of an alcoholic liquid. Here again, the salad maker has ample room to play as opposed to the days of yore when cider or distilled vinegars were the only major choices.

Wine vinegars offer a range from the delicacy of champagne vinegar to the robust heartiness of red wine vinegar. The best wine vinegars will retain tones of the wine from which they were prepared. Sherry vinegar from Spain gives foods the rich, aromatic flavor of a fine sherry. Some of the better cider vinegars have a faint but absolute taste of apples, and cane vinegar from the Caribbean and Louisiana has a hint of molasses in its undertones; those from the Caribbean are milder than the Louisiana version.

In Asia, rice vinegars are abundant. Japanese rice wine vinegar is more delicate than the Chinese version, and brown rice vinegar is stronger and darker in hue than lighter versions.

Fruit-infused and -flavored vinegars are also readily available, and range from raspberry to more exotic ones like passionfruit. They can also be prepared easily at home. Depending on the desired pungency of the fruit flavor, place one-half cup of fruit (more if the fruit is subtly flavored) and 1¾ cups of white wine vinegar in a preserving jar. Crush the fruit just to bruise it and release the flavor. Cover and place it in a sunny window for a week so the flavors will infuse. When ready, strain off the liquid into a bottle, seal it, and store it in a dark place.

With all these choices, there's nothing simpler than preparing a basic vinaigrette. A French proverb says that to prepare a salad dressing you need a spendthrift for oil and a miser for vinegar. Most of us use proportions of oil to vinegar that range from three to one, to four to one, depending on the flavor of the oil and the pungency of the vinegar. Salt and pepper to taste, and that's it. You may wish to add a bit of Dijon mustard, or a scant amount of minced garlic, or even a dash of sesame oil.

SALADS AND SLAWS

Basic Green Salad   *Serves 4*

It doesn't get any simpler than this, but on some days it just doesn't get any better than this, either. You can vary the lettuces, the dressings, and even add fresh herbs or edible flowers for a special occasion.

1 medium head Boston lettuce
1 clove garlic, cut in half
Vinaigrette, to taste (see page 68)

Separate, wash, and dry the lettuce leaves and place them into a salad bowl that you have rubbed with the garlic. Drizzle on the vinaigrette, toss, and serve.

Asian Salad   *Serves 4 to 6*

I find I am making this salad more and more when I get to the farmers' market and can find just the right greens. I like the spice and the heat of the combination of mizuna and baby red and green mustard. I use the light soy and rice wine vinaigrette on almost all of my salads in the summer for its cooling taste.

¼ pound baby mizuna leaves (see Note)
¼ pound baby mustard greens (see Note)

For the vinaigrette:
¼ cup low-sodium soy sauce
¼ cup rice wine vinegar
1 teaspoon brown sugar, or to taste
1 tablespoon toasted sesame oil
Salt and freshly ground black pepper, to taste

Wash and dry the salad greens and place them in a bowl. Mix the vinaigrette, taste, and adjust the seasonings with salt and pepper. Drizzle the dressing over the greens, taking care not to drown them. Occasionally, when I'm feeling a bit frisky, I'll add a handful of fresh raspberries.

NOTE: This combination of greens can be replaced by any spicy salad green or Asian greens mix.

Brazilian Okra Salad   *Serves 4 to 6*

Okra is often discounted by those outside of the American South as too slippery to eat. Folks who don't cotton to the mucilaginous pod can take a hint from the Brazilians who take the young vegetable, blanch it, and serve it almost raw and crunchy over crisp lettuce in a salad.

1 head Bibb lettuce
½ pound small, tender okra pods, topped
1 medium tomato, peeled, seeded, and coarsely chopped
Vinaigrette of choice

Wash and dry the lettuce and tear the leaves into bite-sized pieces. Place them in a glass salad bowl. Bring 3 cups of water to a boil in a small saucepan and add the okra. Cook for 2 minutes and then remove and shock in a bath of ice water to stop the cooking process. Drain well and add the okra and the chopped tomato to the salad bowl. Top with your favorite vinaigrette, mix, and serve immediately.

Orange and Radish Salad *Serves 4 to 6*

Moroccan salads are worthy of an entire chapter by themselves. Ranging from the savory to the slightly sweet, they offer a range of flavors. This variation on the classic orange and radish salad combines the sweetness of the orange-flower water, confectioner's sugar, and the oranges with the bite of the grated radish for an unusual but refreshing taste.

6 large red globe radishes
4 large navel oranges
2 tablespoons freshly squeezed orange juice
1½ teaspoons orange-flower water
1 teaspoon confectioners' sugar

Wash the radishes thoroughly. Cut off and discard the green tops and roots and grate or shred the radishes into a glass salad bowl. Peel the oranges and segment them, removing all membrane. Reserve 2 tablespoons of the juice. Place the oranges in the bowl with the grated radish. Mix the orange juice, orange-flower water, and sugar together in a small glass bowl, and pour over the orange and radish mix. Cover with plastic wrap and set aside for 30 minutes so that the flavors mix. Serve at room temperature.

Orzo Salad *Serves 4 to 6*

Orzo is a rice-shaped pasta that is often used in soups. This salad uses orzo instead of rice for an unusual, anytime dish.

3 cups cooked orzo (see Note)
¼ cup chopped flat-leaf parsley
1 cup green peas, cooked
½ teaspoon minced garlic
3 tablespoons olive oil
1 tablespoon balsamic vinegar
Salt and freshly ground black pepper, to taste

Place the cooked orzo into a non-reactive serving bowl. Add the parsley and peas. Prepare a vinaigrette from the remaining ingredients and drizzle it over the salad. Stir to mix well. Cover with plastic wrap and refrigerate for 1 hour. Serve at room temperature.

NOTE: Orzo is readily available in grocery stores. Cook it according to package directions. Half of a 1-pound package (about 1⅓ cups uncooked) will yield 3 cups cooked.

Vinny's Arugula Salad   *Serves 4 (with garlic cloves left over)*

This favorite salad was taught to me by my friend, Vinny Scotto, chef-owner of Gonzo in Greenwich Village in New York.

1 cup peeled whole garlic cloves
Balsamic vinegar to cover
2 bunches arugula
Freshly shaved Parmesan cheese, to taste
Vinaigrette (see page 68), made with the garlic-infused balsamic vinegar
Salt and freshly ground black pepper, to taste

For the garlic cloves:
Remove the hard ends and any blemishes from the garlic cloves and place them in a small, non-reactive saucepan with balsamic vinegar to cover. Bring to a boil. Lower the heat and simmer, stirring occasionally, for 20 minutes or until the vinegar becomes syrupy and the garlic softens. Remove from heat, let cool, and pour into a glass jar. Store in the refrigerator, tightly covered. Use as desired in this salad, or in any other salad. You can use the vinegar, which will be infused with garlic flavor, for the vinaigrette.

For the salad:
Wash and dry the arugula and remove any tough stems and discolored spots. Place the arugula in a glass salad bowl with 3 tablespoons of the garlic cloves. Sprinkle with as much cheese as you'd like, and drizzle with garlic-infused balsamic vinaigrette. Season with salt and pepper, mix gently, and serve.

NOTE: You'll have enough garlic to make this salad several times. The garlic will keep in a tightly closed jar in the refrigerator for about a month.
   If the balsamic vinegar is too sharp, you may wish to add about ¼ teaspoon of Demerara sugar to the vinaigrette.

Katchumber *Serves 6*

Although it can be served as a side salad, in India this mix of chopped vegetables is traditionally eaten as a condiment along with chutneys, pickles, and relishes.

1 cup seeded green bell pepper, chopped into ½-inch dice
1 cup onion, chopped into ½-inch dice
2 large tomatoes, peeled, seeded, and coarsely chopped (about 1½ cups)
2 teaspoons minced cilantro
1 tablespoon freshly squeezed lemon juice
Freshly ground black pepper to taste

Place the green pepper, onion, and tomatoes in a non-reactive bowl. Add the cilantro and lemon juice, and mix thoroughly. Cover with plastic wrap and chill for at least 1 hour. Add a few grindings of black pepper and serve chilled.

Spinach Salad *Serves 4*

This contemporary classic is served in a variety of different ways. I like mine with mushrooms and red onion, and a warm dressing made with some of the drippings from the bacon.

1 pound baby spinach leaves
2 medium mild red onions, thinly sliced
1½ cups thinly sliced cremini mushrooms
5 strips bacon, cut into 1-inch pieces
2 tablespoons olive oil
2 teaspoons brown sugar, or to taste
1 tablespoon red wine vinegar
Salt and freshly ground black pepper

Wash the spinach leaves thoroughly, dry them, and place them in a non-reactive bowl. Add the onions and the mushrooms. Fry the bacon until crisp. Pour off all but 1 tablespoon of the rendered fat, add the olive oil and sugar, and continue to cook for 1 minute. Rapidly stir in the vinegar. Add salt and pepper, adjust the seasonings, and pour the hot dressing over the spinach. Mix gently. Serve immediately.

Hearts of Palm Salad   *Serves 4*

I discovered hearts of palm in Brazil where they appear in many salads. You can gobble down all you want at the salad bars in churrascarias, restaurants where the main attraction is an unending procession of spit-roasted meats carved at your table. In Brazil, I also learned that the best way with hearts of palm is the simplest way.

1 (14-ounce) can hearts of palm
1 small head Boston lettuce
1 small Vidalia onion, thinly sliced
Vinaigrette (see page 68)

Drain the hearts of palm in a colander and pick off and discard any hard pieces. Cut the hearts of palm into 1-inch rounds. Wash, dry, and pick over the lettuce, discarding any bruised or brown spots. Tear the leaves into bite-size pieces and place the leaves and the hearts of palm in a medium salad bowl. Add the onion slices and vinaigrette and toss. Serve immediately.

Mom's Cole Slaw *Serves 4 to 6*

My mother was a purist about her cole slaw and did not include many of the other additions that turn up in some slaws. Hers simply used green cabbage and occasionally a bit of red cabbage for variety and color.

1 small green cabbage, cored and shredded
½ small red cabbage, cored and shredded
½ cup mayonnaise
2 tablespoons cider vinegar
Sugar, to taste
Salt and freshly ground black pepper, to taste

Place the cabbages in a medium glass bowl and fluff with a fork so that the shreds are separated. Mix the mayonnaise, cider vinegar, and sugar together in a small bowl and pour it over the cabbage. Season with salt and pepper, cover with plastic wrap, and place in the refrigerator for at least 1 hour so that the flavors mix. When ready to serve, adjust the seasonings and serve chilled.

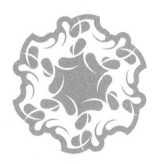

COLE SLAW

While it may seem as American as the apple pie that it sometimes precedes, cole slaw is a term that comes to us from the Dutch word *koolsla* (a composite word formed from *kool*, meaning cabbage and *sla*, an abbreviated one meaning salad). Cole slaw was first written about in the U.S. in a 1794 as "cold slaw," but the true term only came into usage in 1842. The resulting confusion means that some folks think slaw is the term and cold is the adjective, so they refer to cold slaws and hot slaws. However, "cole" meant cabbage in England (as in "colewort greens," which in the South was corrupted into collard greens). Greens, though, are not the only ingredients, and most modern slaws add such ingredients as carrots or raisins. Some chefs really go wild, adding ingredients like jicama, julienne of bell pepper, and radishes. There are three basic types of cole slaw dressings: one that places the accent on vinegar, another that uses mayonnaise, and a third boiled dressing like an egg-yolk enriched white sauce.

Wilma Peterson's Famous
Nationwide Favorite Potato Salad *Serves 15 to 20*

(Inspired by her husband, Miles Peterson, and his southern compatriots)

You can do a lighter version with mayonnaise and no eggs, but so help me, if you've had the protein-rich variety, the eggless one is just a sad, pale imitation.

5 pounds Idaho potatoes
1 (32-ounce) jar Heinz kosher dill spears, diced (I try not to substitute brands)
1 (16-ounce) jar Heinz sweet pickles, diced
1 (16-ounce) jar green olives with pimentos, diced
1 pretty large yellow onion, diced (important: no one wants big chunks of onion)
1 (32-ounce) jar Miracle Whip (and only Miracle Whip) salad dressing
The smallest jar of Hellmann's mayonnaise you can find, unless you use Hellmann's for other
   things. You'll only need 1 or 2 tablespoons.
6 or 7 hard-boiled eggs

Peel and boil the potatoes (or boil the potatoes and skin them) until they are soft to the center when pierced by a fork. When the potatoes are cool enough, transfer them to a bowl or container big enough to work in and break them into large chunks. Drain any excess juice that may have accumulated around the pickles and olives and add them with the onions. You may want to go lighter on the pickles and olives at first because they are both strong flavors, adding to taste later on in the process. With a large wooden spoon or similar utensil, mix the potatoes and other ingredients well, breaking up the potatoes some more as you mix.

Once the ingredients are well mixed, add the Miracle Whip a few large spoonfuls at a time. The key to dressing the salad is to make it moist and flavorful without drowning it. Keep adding the Miracle Whip until it starts making that sound when you mix it. If you are an experienced cook who has ever mixed hamburger meat with eggs for meatloaf, you know what sound I mean; I can't describe it in words. Then add just one or maybe two tablespoons of Hellmann's mayonnaise.

Finally, cut the hard-boiled eggs in quarters directly into the bowl. Mix them in until the potato salad starts to turn a light golden color, about three minutes.

In my opinion, the salad is best after about a good hour or so of refrigeration (if you can get it to the refrigerator without a swarm of locusts descending and carrying it away). Others prefer it at room temperature to let the flavor of the sweet and sour pickles and olives "blossom."

POTATO SALAD

Like cole slaw, potato salad is a summer favorite in any African-American household, or any American household for that matter. There are as many variations on the theme of potatoes, seasonings, and mayonnaise as there are grandmothers in the U.S. In 2002, the Southern Foodways Alliance had a contest at its annual symposium, and members were asked to submit recipes. We tasted and tested under tents in the pouring rain, attempting to find the most stellar variants. I left still convinced that my mother's was a winner—I hadn't submitted the recipe in order to give the others a chance (or so I told myself).

This version from my friend, Audrey Peterson, was a finalist. It's loaded with ingredients and is fantastic. The recipe comes complete with the story of how her German mother learned it from her African-American father and succeeded so mightily that she was saddled with the task for life. Sadly Audrey's father left this world in 2001 but the potato salad stands as memorial to his skill as a teacher and to her mother's amazing ability to blend cultures as well as she mixes potato salad. Here it is verbatim.

Patates Douces Vinaigrette   *Serves 4*

This potato salad is eaten in the **French Caribbean** and what makes it different from ordinary potato salad is that the potatoes are the orange sweet potatoes most of us associate with Thanksgiving. Here, the potatoes are served on a bed of lettuce, and dressed with a vinaigrette.

4 medium garnet sweet potatoes
1 small head Boston lettuce
3 scallions, including the green parts, thinly sliced
Vinaigrette (see page 68)

Wash the sweet potatoes and place them in a saucepan with water to cover. Cook them for 15 minutes, or until they are fork-tender. Drain them, allow them to cool, and peel them. Cut the potatoes into ¾-inch dice and reserve. Separate, wash, and dry the lettuce and arrange it on a platter. Top the lettuce with the sweet potatoes, sprinkle with the scallions, and drizzle the vinaigrette over the whole dish. Serve chilled or at room temperature.

Cremini Mushrooms with Lemon Vinaigrette   *Serves 4*

The cremini mushroom, also known as crimini or "Baby Bella," is nothing more than a baby portobello mushroom. I love their meaty texture and their rich taste in salads. This one depends on having the freshest mushrooms, about 2 inches in diameter, with closed caps.

24 cremini mushrooms of uniform size
½ cup freshly shaved Parmesan cheese

Lemon vinaigrette:
1 tablespoon freshly squeezed lemon juice
3 tablespoons extra virgin olive oil
¼ teaspoon grated lemon zest
Pinch of sugar

Slice the mushrooms thinly and arrange them on a platter. Top the mushrooms with the Parmesan cheese. In a small bowl, whisk together the lemon juice, oil, lemon zest, and sugar. Drizzle the vinaigrette over the whole dish. Serve immediately.

Gazpacho *Serves 6*

The picky among you will cry, "But gazpacho is a soup!" Ah yes, I'll reply, but it is a soup that is nothing more than a liquidized salad. Traditionally gazpacho was prepared in stone mortars, and some used to say that when blenders became common in Andalusian kitchens their whirr in the summer was a mighty roar. This is the way it was served in Andalusia in the 1970s when my parents and I would summer on the Costa del Sol and enjoy it at a small restaurant in Fuengirola called Easo. Some recipes allow that the garnishes are optional. As far as I am concerned, they are obligatory, so chop away.

2 large slices of stale country bread, crusts removed
1 small onion, cut into chunks
2 garlic cloves, coarsely chopped
2 tablespoons olive oil
1 small cucumber, peeled, seeded, and coarsely chopped
1 medium red bell pepper, seeded and coarsely chopped
5 large summer-ripe tomatoes, peeled, seeded, and coarsely chopped
1 tablespoon red wine or sherry vinegar
Salt and freshly ground black pepper, to taste

For the garnishes:
1 small cucumber, peeled, seeded, and cut into ¼-inch dice
1 small green bell pepper, seeded and cut into ¼-inch dice
1 small onion, cut into ¼-inch dice
4 tablespoons croutons prepared from cubes of country bread fried in olive oil

Place the bread in a medium bowl with water to cover and allow it to soak for a few minutes. Remove the bread, squeeze out the water, and place the bread in a blender with the onion, garlic, and olive oil. Blend the mixture until a paste forms. Add the cucumber, bell pepper, tomatoes, red wine vinegar, and 2 cups of water, and blend until all of the ingredients are pulverized. (You may have to do it in two batches.) Place the soup in a bowl, cover it tightly with plastic wrap, and refrigerate it for 12 hours.

To serve, remove the soup from the refrigerator, correct the seasonings with salt and pepper, and dilute it with cold water, if necessary. Pour the soup in a tureen and serve it cold, surrounded by the garnishes. Diners add their favorites to their bowls.

Cucumber-Tomato *Raita*   *Serves 4*

In India the mixture of vegetables and yogurt known as *raita* is a condiment used to temper the heat of spicier dishes. Mixtures include cooked potatoes spiced with garam masala; tomatoes and scallions; bell peppers, and other vegetables. The dish depends only on the inventiveness of the chef.

1 cup unflavored yogurt
1 small ripe tomato, peeled, seeded, and coarsely chopped
½ cucumber, peeled, seeded, and cut into ¼-inch dice
1 scallion, including 3 inches of the green part, thinly sliced
½ teaspoon red pepper flakes
½ chiltecpin chilli, seeded and minced, or to taste (see Note, page 120)

Mix all the ingredients together in a small, non-reactive bowl. Cover and place in the refrigerator for at least 1 hour to allow the flavors to mingle. Serve chilled.

Jamaican Cucumber Salad   *Serves 6*

I've spent a lot of time poking around in the kitchen of my Jamaican girlfriend, Maria Williams-Jones. At her home I discovered boiled green bananas, brown lemonade, and more. No discovery came with quite the same startling effect as her cucumber salad. Seeing a salad that looked very much like my mother's cucumber salad, I took a forkful and had no sooner swallowed the first bite when I began to splutter and cough. "Oh," said Maria, hearing my cries of distress, "I forgot that you weren't Jamaican." Actually, I am used to eating hot foods; it was just the element of surprise. The dish looked so similar to my mother's summer salad that I didn't notice the extra kick of minced Scotch Bonnet pepper until it was in my mouth. Now I proceed with caution whenever I poke around in the fridge and Maria, good friend that she is, goes a bit lighter on the chilli.

3 large cucumbers, peeled and very thinly sliced
2 medium Vidalia onions, thinly sliced
4 allspice berries, cracked
⅓ cup Jamaican cane vinegar (see Note)
2 tablespoons brown sugar, or to taste
½ Scotch Bonnet chilli, seeded and minced, or to taste (see Note, page 120)

Alternately layer the cucumbers and onions in a medium glass bowl. Place the allspice, vinegar, sugar, and chilli together in a small bowl and whisk until well mixed. Pour the sweetened vinegar over the cucumbers. Place a plate directly on the salad in the bowl, weight the plate with a 1-pound can, and refrigerate for 3 hours. When ready to serve, remove the weight and plate, fluff the salad with a fork, and serve chilled. Don't forget to warn your guests about the chilli!

NOTE: See Mail Order Sources, page 199.

North African Lemon and Olive Salad

This salad of lemons and olives is one of the small plates that come to the table as an appetizer in North Africa. A similar Sicilian salad plays with the mixture of oranges and olives, but I prefer the tart brightness of this one. I've added another layer of flavor with the smoky undertones of the *pimentón*.

3 large Meyer lemons (see Note)

¼ cup sea salt

1 teaspoon *pimentón*

1 teaspoon ground cumin

¼ teaspoon sugar

2 tablespoons finely minced Vidalia onion

4 tablespoons chopped flat-leaf parsley

4 tablespoons extra virgin olive oil

30 Moroccan violet or substitute black olives, pitted and minced

2 sprigs flat-leaf parsley, for garnish

Peel the lemons and soak them in salted water (3 cups water, ¼ cup sea salt) for an hour and a half. Remove and drain thoroughly. Remove and discard zest and membrane. Mince the flesh and place it in a medium bowl. Add the *pimentón*, cumin, sugar, onion, and chopped parsley, and drizzle in the olive oil. Mix gently. Cover with plastic wrap and chill for at least 1 hour. Before serving, top with the minced olives and garnish with the parsley sprigs.

NOTE: Meyer lemons are winter fruits that are believed to be a cross between a lemon and an orange. Originally from China, they have a sweet flavor that is quite different from that of an ordinary lemon. Look for firm, plump lemons with no bruises. They will last in the refrigerator for 2 to 3 days. They are available in gourmet markets from November through March.

Pimentón is a Spanish spice, also known as smoked paprika. It is made by grinding smoke-dried peppers.

Chapter 3

PICKLES AND SALSAS

Salting, smoking, and pickling are among the oldest forms of food preservation. No one can actually document when pickling began. The English word pickle comes to us from the Middle English *pikkyll,* which in turn is from the Middle Dutch *pekel* and perhaps related to the German *pokel,* meaning to brine. The word *pickle,* in fact, is one of the few culinary terms like barbecue that can be a noun, verb, or an adjective. The most reliable theory is that pickling was one of those happy culinary accidents that occurred when an ingredient came into contact with some old wine that had turned into vinegar.

Wine residue has been found in vessels that date back to 3000 B.C. Wine was certainly used by the Mesopotamians and the Egyptians, where it was loved by the aristocracy of the former and used in religious ritual by the latter. It's mentioned by Hippocrates in the fifth century B.C. and lauded for its medicinal uses. The Greeks had vineyards and kept their wine in pottery flasks sealed with clay and wax. It's a certainty that when one or more of the seals was broken, vinegar was virtually a guaranteed result, so vinegar has a long culinary history as well. As goes vinegar, so come pickles.

Humankind has been putting together cucumbers, spices, salt, and brine for a long time. It's been documented that Cleopatra ate pickles thinking that they would contribute to her beauty and health, and pickles were one of the foods issued to Roman legions. Pickles, though, are more than simply cucumbers and brine. Perhaps the most famous pickle of the ancient world was the Roman *garum.*

Food historians who study classical Rome have spent a great deal of time debating the taste and consistency of *garum.* The clear sauce was so beloved by the ancient Romans that it was everywhere and could be considered the ketchup of its day. Unlike ketchup, though, it was extremely expensive and priced more like today's white truffles.

There were two basic types of the sauce available. The less expensive version of the sauce, called *muria,* was prepared from inferior fish mixed with a thick brine, seasoned with oregano, and cooked until the fish parts liquefied. Reduced wine was added and the sauce allowed to cool. It was then strained and served when clear. *Garum* was the more expensive of the two and was prepared from the entrails of mackerel. Aristocrats ate an even more extravagant version prepared from the livers of red mullet. This was so expensive that Pliny commented on its excess, judgmentally naming it *garum sociorum* and saying, "Marcus Apicius, who was born with a genius for every kind of extravagance, considered it an excellent practice for mullet to be killed in a sauce made from their companions." Hence the name *garum sociorum* (meaning companion *garum*). The liquid may have tasted like the fish sauces consumed in the Far East today: *nam pla* in Thailand, *nuoc mam* in Vietnam, *tuk trey* in Cambodia, and *patis* in the Philippines.

Fish prices were regulated and the cost of *garum* rose and fell with the availability of certain types of fish. Eventually the situation got so out of hand that Tiberius Caesar imposed sumptuary taxes on red mullet, much like today's luxury taxes. There were still those who couldn't do without it.

Inelegantly put, the more costly versions of the sauce were prepared from fish guts. In one version, mackerel blood, intestines, and gills were placed into an open vessel and then covered with salt. Vinegar, parsley, and wine were added to the mix. It was also flavored with sweet herbs such as oregano, mint, basil, thyme, lovage (a celery relative), chervil, sweet cicely, and fennel. There were different brews of *garum,* with different cities offering a liquid with its own specific combination of tastes. Some of the better-known ones came from Pompeii, Leptis, Magnus, and Antipolis (today's Antibes). Each had its partisans, but no Roman epicure was more entranced with the more expensive versions of the sauce than Marcus Apicius, the gourmet and culinarian whose recipes were collected in a work entitled *De Re Coquinaria,* one of the earliest cookbooks.

In fact, there were three individuals who went by the name Apicius. The second of them was the wealthy and decadent gourmet whose extravagant ways with matters culinary resulted in the name Apicius itself becoming a cliché for wealth. Pilloried by later writers for his excesses, he was noted for his love of exotic varieties of the sauce that occasionally seemed to take on the sophistication of the eating of Japanese *fugu,* which if improperly prepared can be lethal. Martial, another Roman poet gives a hint:

> Take this gift, the proud sauce
> that's made from the first blood
> of a still breathing mackerel.

While *garum* and *muria* were certainly the most famous of the Roman pickles, other pickles existed. Apicius mentions several, including pickles made from vegetables from all over the empire. The Romans pickled lettuce leaves, turnips, asparagus, fennel, and onions as well as apricots, lemons, and peaches from the far-flung outreaches of the colonies in Africa and Asia Minor. The basic Roman pickle was prepared in a brine of vinegar, olive oil, and salt, with honey used as a sweetener. (Sugar from cane would only arrive in the eastern Mediterranean in the seventh century A.D., after the fall of the empire.) When the empire fell, the taste for *garum* faded with it, except for a brief time when hints of the fishy taste were preserved in the cooking of Byzantium.

In addition to heading east to Byzantium, the pickling traditions of the Roman Empire went underground in Europe and survived, along with other remnants of the wisdom of the classical world, in the convents and monasteries of medieval Europe. By the thirteenth century, the medieval princely households were again making pickles. The large kitchens offered a variety of recipes for pickles using wine vinegar and verjuice. *Compost,* a 1393 recipe from Goodman of Paris, is a pickle that took four months of preparation and included walnuts, carrots, pears, peaches, and fennel among its ingredients.

The discoveries of the Age of Exploration brought other ingredients into the pickling pots. Salad savant and gourmet John Evelyn included pickle recipes in his culinary treatises, including a mango of pickles that is similar to a cucumber pickle but with mustard. A 1694 recipe for "pickle lila, an Indian pickle" is an early hint of the development of the piccalilli tradition that developed as Europe became acquainted with the pickling traditions of the subcontinent and the East.

On the Indian subcontinent, inhabitants of southern India had nibbled on pickled mango pieces since the Harappan days (3200–2000 B.C.). The *achars* and lime pickles of the region traveled first with the explorers and later with the colonials to become a part of the European diet from the seventeenth century onward. Pickles certainly have had their place in the foods of the Islamic world and turn up everywhere, from the preserved lemons used to flavor tajines and other dishes in Morocco, to the seasoned olives on virtually every Mediterranean table. Ancient Persia also evidenced a fondness for sweet-and-sour flavors including a love for the turnip pickles which can still be found today. In the Far East, Chinese royal kitchens in the second century B.C. employed 2,271 individuals, including sixty-two pickle and sauce chefs. With the arrival of colonists in the Americas, the pickling traditions of Europe and the Middle and Far East arrived in the New World.

Amerigo Vespucci was a pickle dealer in Seville before he became an explorer and gave his name to a continent that has become a home to all of the pickles of the world in the twenty-first century. The United States has its own lengthy pickle history that includes founding father Thomas Jefferson waxing eloquent on them, stating, "on a hot day in Virginia, I know of nothing more comforting than a fine spiced pickle, brought up troutlike from the sparkling depths of the aromatic jar below the stairs in Aunt Sally's cellar."

Jefferson's fishing expedition in the pickle jar is only a part of the country's fascination with pickles and pickling that continues to this day. The cooks of colonial Charleston put up the bounty of their Carolina homes and of the world that came to the city's docks, as artichoke relish, piccalillis, chowchows, pickled okra, and dilly beans. They also transplanted the culinary traditions of Southeast Asia in a pickle known locally as *ats jaar,* which takes its name from either the Indian *achar* or the *achards* of the Caribbean. The turmeric-hued pickle is the classic side to a dish of country captain according to my friend Hoppin' John Taylor. There are the pickles of the Pennsylvania Dutch, the mustard pickles of North Carolina, and the bread-and-butter pickles and crisp watermelon chips that turn up in larders and farmers' markets of the Deep South. They also turn up in the larders of the North where folks like my mother would remember their southern upbringing each summer and fall, and head to the top of the kitchen cabinet to get out the canning pot and jars.

One of my earliest family food memories is of holidays at my maternal grandmother's house and my delight in the pickled Seckel pears and spiced peaches she would prepare. My own mother was noted for her green tomato relish. One year we labored lengthily in our summer house on Martha's Vineyard, trying to capture the exact spice mix of Grandma Jones's pears and peaches. Since then, no summer is complete unless I return with one or more boxes of carefully wrapped jars of my own tomato chutney (but more about that in chapter 4).

I'm old enough to remember when the corner store had a pickle barrel and the pickles cost two cents. I adored them; there was something immensely satisfying about the combination of salty and sour that appealed to my taste buds. By the time I became a preteen, the pickles were packed in plastic and the price had gone up to a nickel. Recently I've found a shop where there is again a pickle barrel, a shop which sells the crisp and garlicky half-sours I remember from my New York City childhood. In my pickling life, the half-sours and kosher dills of my childhood—a gift of the city's Eastern European Jewish population—I leave to the professionals. In the marrow of my bones, I know I can't produce a pickle like the folks at Guss' Pickles, on Orchard Street on Manhattan's Lower East Side, and I wouldn't want to. There's something about the ethos of the professional pickle barrel that I wouldn't want to lose. Rather, I try to capture the homemade pickled ginger of Asia and the pickled okra of the South. There's also the kimchi of the Koreans and the pickled turnips of the Levant. I don't do olives either. Near where I live in Brooklyn, a Middle Eastern shop, Sahadi's, sells a staggering array of pickles and olives, including preserved lemons in a chilli sauce, France's Picholine olives, crunchy pickled turnips from the Middle East, and the fat Cerignola olives from Sicily that are my current favorites. And I've been known to carry more than one jar of *achards* and *piment confit* back on the plane from the Caribbean with the tops tightly sealed with duct tape. When I shop and explore the shelves at the delis all over the country, it seems at times that while we're certainly not a melting pot, we're the pickle barrel of my youth—all of us swimming around in a common love for a seemingly infinite variety of things pickled.

PICKLES AND SALSAS

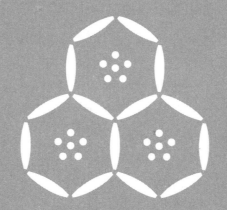

Preserved Lemons *Makes 6 lemons*

These lemons are one of the most memorable flavors of Moroccan cooking. They turn up in everything from slow-cooked tajines to brightly flavored salads. They are simple to prepare and can easily become a larder staple. I like preparing them with the Meyer lemons which have a slightly sweet edge to them, but you can use whatever is available in your local market.

6 large Meyer lemons (see Note, page 89)
¼ cup sea salt
Freshly squeezed lemon juice

With a sharp knife, slice the lemons into quarters, leaving the stem end intact so that they hold together. Rub 2 teaspoons of the salt into the flesh of each lemon, re-form it, and place it in the canning jar. Continue until all lemons have been salted. Press down on the lemons as you add them to the jar to release their juice. Fill the jar with lemon juice to cover, leaving a bit of space before sealing. Let the lemons cure in a warm, dry space for about a month. When ready to use, remove them carefully from the jar with a clean fork. The rest should be refrigerated and will keep for several months. Rinse and add them to your favorite Moroccan dish.

This is the traditional Moroccan version. A Moroccan Jewish version of the lemons is also popular, using a bit of olive oil in the liquid that covers the lemons.

NOTE: Any lemons used for preserving should be organically grown and not treated with chemicals.

Tunisian Lemons in Oil   *Makes 6 lemons*

I have a thing for lemons. I love them just about any way they can be prepared. When I moved to New Orleans, I was thrilled to learn that the climate would allow me to grow my own. Now I spend an inordinate amount of time trying to find new varieties to grow at my house there. Several years ago when I discovered Meyer lemons, I was just about in heaven. They are not only perfect for the preserved lemons that work so well in the cooking of Morocco, they are also grand in this quicker Tunisian version of the pickle. If you can't find Meyer lemons, you can use whatever is available in your market.

6 Meyer lemons (see Note, page 89)
6 cloves garlic, peeled and crushed
1 tablespoon coarse sea salt
1 teaspoon ground coriander seed
¼ teaspoon ground cumin
Extra virgin olive oil

Wash and dry the lemons. Cut them into thin slices over a non-reactive bowl, reserving the juice. Remove any seeds. Add the garlic, salt, coriander, and cumin to the bowl and mix well with a wooden spoon. Cover the bowl with plastic wrap and allow the lemons to sit for at least 5 hours. Layer the marinated lemon slices in a sterilized canning jar, pour olive oil to cover, and shake the jar so that the lemons are well covered. (You may want to give them a poke or two with the back of a wooden spoon to make sure that the oil goes all the way through.) Close the jar tightly and allow it to sit in a cool, dark spot for a week. Serve the lemons with grilled meats or add to dishes.

After opening, refrigerate the remaining lemons. They will keep for several months.

NOTE: Any lemons that are used for preserving should be organically grown and not treated with chemicals.

Oumar's Pickled Okra *Makes about 2 pints*

Of all the vegetables in my life, the one that I know best and eat because I love it is okra. I know that I eat it because I love it and because as a child I was never forced to eat it, since my mother couldn't stand it herself. One of my great sources of culinary pride is that I even managed to get my mother to eat okra, although she never became as much of a fan as I am. It's somehow not surprising that the man in my life, Oumar, is also a pod person. Because he is from Senegal, I would have expected him to love the cooked okra that turns up in dishes like *soupikandia,* but imagine my surprise when I realized that his favorite way with okra was the plain old southern pickled okra, albeit fired up with a bit of habanero chilli. This recipe is the result of the meeting of our two worlds: an okra pickle that combines the flavors of West Africa and the American South.

1 pound small, young okra
½ habanero chilli, thinly sliced (see Note, page 120)
1 small onion, thinly sliced
2 cloves garlic, thinly sliced
3 cups distilled white vinegar
1 tablespoon pickling spice
2 teaspoons salt

Wash the okra and pick over carefully. Discard any pods that are soft or blemished or too mature and woody. Remove any excess at the stem end of the okra pod, being careful not to cut into the pod itself. Place the chilli, onion, garlic, vinegar, pickling spice, salt, and 1 cup of water in a non-reactive saucepan and bring them to a boil over medium heat. Pack the okra into 2 hot sterilized pint canning jars with the stem ends down. Remove the liquid from the heat and slowly pour it over the okra in the jars, dividing it equally between both jars. Seal the jars according to proper canning procedures (see Note, page 103), allow them to cool, and then store them in a cool place for 4 weeks. The pickle is then ready to be served with any grilled or roasted meat, poultry, or fish, or just nibbled by itself as Oumar does.

Watermelon Rind Pickles   *Makes about 4 pints*

I once had a photograph taken with my hand on a watermelon that was draped in kente cloth and posed majestically on a polished brass tray. *The New York Times,* for whom the photograph was taken, didn't use it; they felt that the image was too controversial. Watermelon just has that way about it. Actually, watermelon has been my *bête noire* for much of my life. While I enjoy an occasional taste of the ruby fruit from time to time, I really am not that fond of it in any manner befitting its totemic importance in African-American culinary history. I've tried to eat more, but somehow a slice or two will do me just fine for the summer. I enjoy a seed-spitting contest as much as the next person and I have even learned how to make a wicked watermelon *agua fresca* that's a fine summer cooler.

I go nuts not for the melon itself, but for the rind. I love watermelon rind pickles. I love them so much I wish they'd make a melon that had more instead of less rind so that I wouldn't have to work my way through the meat each summer just to get enough to make my pickles.

9 cups cubed watermelon rind
½ cup salt
1¾ cups cider vinegar
½ cup balsamic vinegar
2 cups dark brown sugar
1 lemon, thinly sliced
2 sticks cinnamon, crushed
1 teaspoon whole cloves
2 teaspoons allspice berries, cracked

Prepare the watermelon rind by removing the green skin and all but a small amount of the red meat. Cut the rind into 1-inch cubes. Place the prepared rind in a large bowl and soak it overnight in a brine prepared from the salt and 2 quarts of water.

When ready to make the pickles, drain the watermelon, wash it with fresh water, and drain it again. Place the rind in a large non-reactive saucepan with water to cover and simmer for 15 minutes or until it is fork-tender. Combine the vinegars, sugar, lemon, cinnamon, cloves, allspice, and 2 cups of water in a second large non-reactive saucepan and bring to a boil. Lower the heat and simmer for 15 minutes, or until you have a thin syrup. Drain the watermelon rind, add it to the syrup, and continue to simmer about 10 to 15 minutes, or until the rind becomes translucent. Place the pieces in hot sterilized jars, cover them with the unstrained syrup, and seal them according to proper canning procedures (see Note). The pickle will keep for several months (if it lasts that long).

NOTE: There are several books that discuss processing and canning procedures far better than I can. An excellent resource is *www.homecanning.com*.

Matt's Lemon-Ginger Watermelon Pickles

Makes about 4 pints

This is my friend Matt Rowley's version of the watermelon pickle that I so dote on. I like the lemony take of his recipe. I've included it verbatim so that you can understand just how crazy my friends are about pickles.

Here's my take on the classic. I've tried it with pickling lime and just don't care for it as much. These stay plenty crisp enough without the lime and are much less of pain. I don't bother peeling the ginger since it's just there, like the lemon, for flavor, anyhow. The real trick is finding a melon with a thick enough rind. When all I have is the modern varieties, I cut the rind into longish (2- to 3-inch) strips rather than the cubish chunks I'd otherwise cut. (Technique tip: It's easiest to trim away the green skin with a peeler before cutting the rind into chunks.)

I suppose I should process these, but I just pack them into plastic one-quart tubs with airtight lids and toss them into the fridge. And I will eat them standing over the sink with a pair of chopsticks.

8 cups of watermelon rind, white parts only, cut into small chunks
Kosher salt
4 cups sugar
2 cups cider vinegar
12 whole cloves (approximately)
2 to 3 cinnamon sticks, about 3 inches long
2 small lemons, scrubbed and sliced into paper-thin rounds
A finger's length of ginger, sliced into coins

Generously salt the rind chunks and chill in a colander set inside a stainless-steel or glass bowl overnight. Rinse and drain. Place the rinds in a non-reactive pot, cover in water, and bring to a boil. Boil for 10 minutes. Drain in a colander but do not rinse. Add the sugar, vinegar, cloves, cinnamon, lemon, and ginger to the pot and bring to a boil. Add the chunks and boil for about another 10 minutes. Process according to traditional canning procedures (see Note, page 103).

Pickled Garlic *Makes about 2 pints*

This is a slightly sweeter version of a recipe that is Persian in origin. In that country, the pickled garlic is served as an accompaniment to dishes or used when fresh garlic is not available.

3 cups cider vinegar
2 cups balsamic vinegar
1 tablespoon sugar
2 pounds garlic, separated into cloves and peeled

Pour the vinegars and sugar into a non-reactive saucepan and bring to a boil over medium heat. Boil for 3 minutes, remove it from the heat, and allow it to cool. Blanch the garlic by plunging it into boiling water for 1 minute and then draining it. Shock the garlic by placing it in a bowl full of ice cubes to stop the cooking process; drain it again and place it in sterilized jars. Pour in the vinegar, making sure that the garlic is well covered. (You may weight the garlic by placing a can or weight on top of it to make sure that all of the garlic is submerged.) After all of it is submerged, seal the jars and allow them to sit for 1 month.

Piment Confit *Makes about 5 cups*

The markets in Martinique and Guadeloupe are a delight for any food lover. There, women with multicolored madras head ties vie for customers' attention with their bright arrays of fruits and vegetables. There are bunches of leeks, carrots, and seasonings for soup, a wide assortment of leafy greens, gourds and calabashes and Day-glo orange pumpkins. Guavas are piled next to pineapples and fruits like Barbados cherries and passion fruit that mean the tropics to me. I'm always drawn to the area of the market where spices are sold and women bring in the fruit and vegetables that they've put up at home. There, I indulge in syrups of hog plums and sorrel, special mixes of *Colombo* or curry, and the *piment confits* that are the French islands' special way with hot chillies.

10 habanero chillies, cut in half lengthwise and seeded
   (see Note, page 120)
1 cup carrot sticks, cut lengthwise
1 cup string beans, topped and tailed
1 cup cauliflower florets
10 small shallots, peeled
2 teaspoons cracked black peppercorns
3 cups cane vinegar, or more to cover
   (see Mail Order Sources, page 199)

Place the chillies in a large, sterilized jar. Blanch the carrots, string beans, cauliflower, and shallots by placing them in boiling water for 1 minute, draining them, and shocking them in ice water to stop the cooking process. Drain the vegetables and arrange them with the chillies in the jar. Cover the vegetables with the peppercorns and vinegar. Add more vinegar if the vegetables are not covered. Cover the jar and store it in a cool place to allow the vegetables to marinate for at least 24 hours before serving. Eat them at you own risk; they will be hot and will get hotter. When they're gone, use the spicy vinegar to add heat to soups, stews, and marinades.

Kimchi *About 2 pints*

This pickle is a Korean basic, and rapidly becoming a favorite in New York City where Korean-owned delis are a part of life. Thick leaves of bok choy covered in a peppery sauce are a common sight, with each store having its own variation ranging from mild to tongue-numbing. As folks select and compare their favorites, the condiment has become one of the newest tastes of the city.

1 head bok choy, stalks chopped and green leaves shredded
3 tablespoons salt
1 teaspoon hot chilli powder
1 tablespoon minced garlic
3 scallions, including 1 inch of the green part, minced
1 tablespoon sugar
1 thumb-sized piece ginger, peeled and grated

Place the bok choy in a large non-reactive bowl, add the salt, and allow it to sit overnight. The next day, rinse the bok choy with cold water. Drain it, pat it dry, and place it in a large crock. Add the chilli powder, garlic, scallions, sugar, and ginger, and stir to make sure that all of the ingredients are well mixed. Place a plate directly on top of the mixture and weight for an hour or so. Remove the plate and the weight, cover the crock loosely, and let the bok choy marinate for about four days. (The warmer the room, the shorter the time the kimchi will need.) When the cabbage is soft and slightly transluscent, chill, and then serve. The remainder should be refrigerated in a sealed container.

Souskai   *Serves 4*

This way of serving green fruit in a chilli-and-lime juice marinade comes from the islands of the Indian Ocean, but it has been taken to the hearts and stomachs of those in the French Antilles who now claim it as their own.

4 firm green mangoes
2 scallions, including 2 inches of the green part, minced
1 clove garlic, minced
1 small, ripe tomato, peeled, seeded, and minced
1 habanero chilli, or to taste, seeded and minced (see Note, page 120)
Freshly squeezed juice of 3 limes
Salt and freshly ground black pepper, to taste

Peel the mangoes, cut them into ¾-inch dice, and place them in a non-reactive bowl. Add the scallions, garlic, tomato, chilli, lime juice, and salt and pepper, and stir to make sure it is well mixed. Cover with plastic wrap and refrigerate for at least 1 hour, stirring occasionally. Drain and serve in the chilled liquid, skewered on toothpicks.

Coconut *Souskai*   *Serves 4*

Coconut is also made into *souskai*, but it is eaten with its marinade. Remind your guests to take care not to bite down on a piece of chilli.

½ coconut, shelled and peeled
1 teaspoon salt
1 clove garlic, minced
1 habanero chilli, minced (See Note, page 120)
Freshly squeezed juice of 2 limes

Cut the coconut into long strips with a vegetable peeler and place the strips in a medium non-reactive bowl. Prepare a marinade with the salt, garlic, chilli, and lime juice, and pour it over the coconut strips. Cover the bowl with plastic wrap and allow the *souskai* to marinate for at least an hour at room temperature. When ready to serve, bring out toothpicks and allow the guests to spear the coconut strips directly from the marinade.

Easy English Pickles   *Makes about 2 pints*

This is a variant of a recipe I discovered in an English pamphlet on how to make soups, sauces, pickles, and chutneys. I can't find a date for it, but the language and the graphics and the fact that it cost tuppence *(2d)* make me suspect that it may date from the 1930s. The recipe is simple, surprisingly spicy, and is perhaps a remnant of England's colonial legacy.

2 cups cider vinegar
1 teaspoon salt
2 teaspoons dark brown sugar
1 jalapeño chilli, minced, or to taste (see Note, page 120)
1 pound Granny Smith apples, peeled, cored, and coarsely chopped
1 pound Vidalia onions, peeled and thinly sliced

Place the vinegar, salt, sugar, and chilli in a non-reactive saucepan. Add the apples and onions and bring the mixture to a boil. Cook for five minutes. Spoon it into canning jars and cover tightly. This is a quick pickle and should be kept refrigerated. If you want to make a large batch, preserve according to proper canning procedures (see page 103).

Barb Peckham's Mustard Pickle   *Makes about 6 pints*

Barb Peckham is my neighbor in Martha's Vineyard. Over the years, we have discovered a mutual love of cooking, canning, and preserving. When I was finishing up this book during the summer on Martha's Vineyard, I mentioned that I could use a few of her good pickling recipes. She arrived the next day with a sheaf of paper that included this recipe from her Grandma Pope, a dyed-in-the-wool Yankee to the marrow of her bones, according to Barb. This mustard pickle is similar to the *ats jaar* of Charleston (see page 160) and some of the relishes known as chow/chow or piccalilli. You can increase the amounts of vegetables to industrial quantities as in the original recipe, or make smaller quantities as in this version.

2 cups small cucumbers, peeled and cut
  into chunks
½ head cauliflower, divided into florets
2 cups small green tomatoes, quartered
2 cups pearl onions, peeled
1 small red bell pepper, cut into chunks
2 cups string beans, topped, tailed, and cut
  into 2-inch pieces
1 small heart celery, cut into chunks
1 cup salt
4 cups distilled white vinegar
1 tablespoon all-purpose flour
½ cup sugar, or to taste
1 tablespoon dry mustard powdered, or to taste
¼ teaspoon turmeric mixed with cold vinegar

Soak the cucumbers, cauliflower, tomatoes, onions, pepper, beans, and celery overnight in water to cover mixed with 1 cup of salt. The next day, drain the vegetables. Cover them with fresh water, blanch, and then drain again before shocking them in ice water. Drain them and pack into sterilized jars. To prepare the pickling liquid, bring the vinegar, flour, sugar, mustard, and turmeric to a boil. Allow it to cool slightly and pour it over the vegetables. Cap, seal, and refrigerate, or process according to canning procedures (see page 103).

Grandma Jones's Pickled Seckel Pears   *Makes about 1 quart*

My mother's mother came from a Virginia tradition of cooking and could "put a hurtin' on a roast." Holidays at her house were always celebrated around a table filled with relatives. I was lucky—my Aunt Lalage would allow me to escape the kids' table, where I was tormented by my older cousins, to sit with the grownups and enjoy the tastes of the wide range of pickled condiments my Grandma Jones always served.

3 pounds Seckel pears
1 (3-inch) cinnamon stick
1 teaspoon whole allspice berries
1 teaspoon whole cloves
1 blade mace
1 thumb-sized piece ginger, peeled and thinly sliced
1 cup sugar
2 cups cider vinegar

Wash the pears and place them in a large, non-reactive saucepan with water to cover. Bring them to a boil, lower the heat, and simmer for 5 minutes. Drain the pears, reserving the liquid, and add enough extra water to make 2 cups. Place the liquid back in the saucepan, add the cinnamon, allspice, cloves, mace, ginger, sugar, and vinegar, and simmer for 5 minutes. Return the pears to the saucepan and cook for 30 minutes. Remove the pears with a non-reactive spoon and place them in a hot sterilized canning jar. Pour the liquid over the pears to within ½-inch of the top. Seal the jar and place it in a cool, dark spot for 1 month to allow the flavors to mix. If you are using more than one jar, be sure that the spices are equally divided between the jars.

Asian Pickled Ginger *Serves 2*

Ginger is used in most of the cuisines of Asia in one form or another. Known as *singabera* in Sanskrit, it turns up in stir fries, glazes, and desserts, and with sushi. In Indonesia, it flavors the coffee known as *Kopi Jahe,* and in the Philippines it turns up as ginger tea or *Salabat.* Called *shoga* in Japan, it is a favorite garnish for sushi. One of the simplest ways it is served is this simple sweet pickle inspired by the Japanese *Hari Shoga.*

1 (3-inch) piece of fresh ginger
2 tablespoons distilled white vinegar
2 tablespoons rice wine vinegar
3 tablespoons sugar
Pinch of red pepper flakes
Salt, to taste

Peel the ginger and cut it into thin julienne strips. Combine the vinegars, sugar, pepper flakes, and salt, stirring well until the sugar is dissolved. Add the ginger, stir, cover, and allow to sit for a half an hour so that the flavors develop. Remove the ginger from the liquid and serve with anything from traditional Japanese dishes to grilled meats.

Oumar's Vinegared Chillies   *Makes about 4 pints*

ON THE SIDE

Oumar's taste for the hot astounds even me; I swear he'd eat chillies for breakfast if he could. One day after a photo shoot when I found myself with several pounds of habaneros and jalapeños, he showed me how to preserve them Senegalese-style so that I could always have some on hand to satisfy my favorite chillihead. I've used the cider and balsamic vinegar because I don't always like the harshness of distilled vinegar, but it is not necessary. You simply need vinegar to cover.

1 pound habanero chillies, cut in half (see Note, page 120)
2 cups cider vinegar
1 cup balsamic vinegar

Place the habaneros in a sterilized canning jar and cover them with the vinegars. Seal the jar tightly and store for a few days for the chillies to flavor the vinegar. When the chillies are used up, the vinegar can be used to add heat to soups, stews, and other dishes.

Pickled Jicama   *Makes about 1½ pints*

My friend, Matt Rowley, is a self-proclaimed pickle practitioner. It was only when writing this book that I discovered that like me, he is a closet pickler who spends evenings and weekends coming up with original twists on traditional recipes. Here's another of the recipes he sent me. This one is an original and comes complete with Matt's own headnote.

> This one keeps very well—good to make in small batches like this, but you could easily bump up the volumes. Stays crunchy and doesn't discolor for at least two weeks in the fridge. Don't know about after that, since we always eat it. When I bring this to work, the warehouse workers—Haitian, Mexican, Puerto Rican, Dominican, and French—snarf it down. I choose to take that as a compliment. I especially like the habanero in this pickle; it gives a fruity, full flavor with a little bite that a lot of other peppers wouldn't do. I love chipotles, for instance, but they wouldn't work here. Jalapeños wouldn't do it justice, either. Especially right from the fridge, the cool floral heat is a reprieve from hot-ass, muggy Philadelphia days.

1 large jicama, about 1½ pounds
1 cup sugar
1 cup distilled white vinegar
1 to 2 habanero chillies, stemmed, seeded, and sliced as thinly as possible (see Note, page 120)
2 teaspoons salt

Bisect the jicama laterally through its bulging middle and peel. Slice into pieces about the size of your small finger. Mix thoroughly with the rest of the ingredients, cover, and set aside in the refrigerator for three days.

Salsas

A love of savory condiments is not solely the province of Europe or Asia. While the Greeks were pickling, the Romans were savoring their stinky *garum,* and the Harappan civilizations were beginning India's long love affair with the mango, a tradition of side condiments was growing in the Americas as well. Here, the Mexicas or Aztecs placed great importance on agriculture and on the commerce of food.

Corn, beans, and squash were the three sisters of the agricultural pantheon, grown along with chayote, cactus *tuna,* bulbs, roots, and mushrooms. All were made into sauces and stews along with the native chillies, and seasoned with native tomatoes, vanilla, oregano, epazote, and other aromatic herbs including the colorant achiote or annatto. Side condiments were used to enhance the taste of the food. It's thought that chillies, tomatoes, squash, and avocados were grown by local peoples as early as 5000 B.C.

When the Europeans arrived in Tenochtitlán, the site of today's Mexico City, they found a bounty of New World ingredients that would, in the space of less than a century, change the food profiles of many of the world's cuisines in what is referred to as the Columbian exchange.

On his second voyage in 1493, in Guadeloupe, Columbus acquainted himself and later the world with such delicacies as *anana,* or pineapple, named for its resemblance to the European pinecone. The Caribs, who lived in other regions of the Caribbean, introduced him and later explorers to *taumalin*—a salsa prepared from crabmeat, a form of sour juice, and chillies—which was used to season other dishes. Cortés, however, had tapped the mother lode of salsa ingredients in the grand market Tlatelolco when he arrived in Central America in 1519.

Laid out precisely, with different sectors devoted to different ingredients, the great market of

Tlatelolco boasted a staggering array of produce and foodstuffs. Tomatoes, *mamey sapotes,* tomatillos, sweet potatoes, jicama, cactus, a rainbow of squashes and chillies, mushrooms, and edible flowers were only some of the bounty. There were also seasonings including *hoja santa* with its distinctive anise taste, epazote, oregano, watercress, and New World variants of purslane and sorrel, along with roots that resembled onions and leeks in taste. Many of these were served up in savory mixtures that are the ancestors of today's salsas.

Fast-forward almost 500 years, and the salsa that intrigued the Spaniards was taking the North American continent by storm. From the most basic Tex-Mex dives, to fast food shops, to elegant haute Mexican eateries, the taste potential of salsas was beginning to be explored. By the end of the 1990s, salsas were the fastest growing food trend in the country, with even the smallest supermarket or deli boasting a section. As cooks discovered just how simple they are to make at home, they set about creating their own personalized salsas with ingredients ranging from classic pre-Columbian ones like avocado, tomato, and an array of chillies, to peaches, apricots, and roasted pineapples!

Some Classic Salsa Ingredients

Avocado
(Persea americana)

Although the fruit was originally seen by Europeans in Jamaica in 1696, it most likely originated in Mexico. Called alligator pear by some, and simply "pear" in Jamaica, it generally goes by the name avocado, the English rendering of the Spanish *aguacate* or *ahuacate,* which in turn come from the Aztec *ahuacatl,* meaning testicle. (You've got to see avocados growing on trees to get the joke.)

There are basically two types of avocados in the United States, indicated by their place of origin (California or Florida), and sub-variants within those types. The smaller California variety is richer and more buttery in taste while the Florida one is large and more watery. For salsas, go with the Hass variety from California or another buttery variety from that state.

Bell Peppers
(See page 39)

Chillies

(Capsicum annuum, Capsicum chinenses, and Capsicum frutescens)

The smaller, hotter members of the Solonaceae family have come out of the culinary closet in the past decades in full force. Most of us now know the difference between a jalapeño and a habanero, and we delight in the spicier end of the culinary spectrum. Chillies have been eaten by people in the Americas since 3300 B.C. and have been prized by them for their ability to bring flavor to dishes. Some that might turn up in your salsa recipes include:

ancho: a dark red dried poblano chilli from Mexico

chiltecpin: a small hot, fresh red or green chilli; it is known in some regions as a bird chilli

chipotle: a hot, smoked, dried jalapeño chilli

guajillo: a deep red-brown dried mirasol chilli from Mexico

habanero and Scotch Bonnet: super hot fresh chillies with a distinctive aftertaste, used in jerk and Caribbean dishes, and in some super-hot salsas

jalapeño: a green chilli available fresh and pickled; the classic salsa chilli

New Mexico or Anaheim: green are available fresh, frozen, and canned; red are used dried in *ristras*

serrano: a thin, green, very hot chilli used fresh in salsas

tabasco: a small hot, fresh fresh or green chilli that is also sometimes known as a bird chilli

NOTE: If you're not used to handling chillies, proceed with extreme caution. Wear rubber gloves and don't touch your eyes at any point in the procedure.

Cilantro

(Coriandrum sativum)

It's a love-it-or-hate-it herb. Cilantro was cultivated in Egypt, and the ancient Greeks used it medicinally. Related to caraway, fennel, dill, and anise, it is also known as Chinese parsley or fresh coriander. Coriander usually refers to the seeds of the plant, while cilantro refers to its leaves. The herb is originally from the Mediterranean basin and made its way to the Americas courtesy of the Spaniards who learned to love it from the Moors.

Cilantro is readily available, but will only keep for a few days in the refrigerator. Bunches with roots will keep marginally longer, but it's best to purchase it as you need it. Look for unblemished leaves. Don't confuse it with flat-leaf parsley, which is a different plant altogether.

Corn
(See page 39)

Limes
(Citrus aurantifolia, Citrus latifolia)

The thorny lime tree is thought to be a native of southern Asia, although folks aren't sure whether India, Malaysia, or someplace in between was the exact origin. The Crusaders brought the fruit to Europe in the thirteenth century but it languished because temperature conditions were not right; limes need tropical heat. The fruit gradually made its way to the Canary Islands and from there, Columbus brought seeds to the Caribbean on his second voyage. Limes thrived in the Caribbean and have become a staple in the region. From there, they spread across the Gulf of Mexico into the Central American mainland where they have become important in Mexican cooking as well. Limes might not have been in Moctezuma's salsa, but they definitely sure turn up in many of today's varieties.

When purchasing, look for plump, heavy limes that have a deep green skin, unless you're in the Caribbean where the skin will be yellow at times. Key limes are a small flavorful variety from Florida that is more like the limes of the Caribbean in taste.

Onions
(Allium cepa)

Onions have been cultivated for over 5,000 years and were given as a tribute to the gods of ancient Egypt. They were also given to the slaves who built the pyramids as part of their daily diet. The circle within circle structure of the plant led it to also become a symbol for eternity and fertility. Laws in Hammurabi's Mesopotamia provided for a ration of onions and bread to be given to citizens in need. Onions were eaten by the ancient Greeks, along with their close cousin, garlic. There was even a section of the market in ancient Greece simply known as *ta skorda*, or the garlic. The ancient peoples of the Americas didn't have onions or garlic. They seasoned their salsas with other roots that were similar in flavor.

Onions should be firm and dry when purchased, and should have crisp outer papery skins. There are mild versions of onions like the famous Vidalia onions of Georgia. Red onions are often added to salsas to bring color as well as their sharpness to the dish.

Tomatoes
(See page 40)

Tomatillos
(Physalis ixocarpa)

The tomatillo, also known as the Mexican husk tomato, has been cultivated in Mexico since the time of the Aztecs. The Aztecs made a distinction between the *xictlitomatl* (red tomato) and the *tomatl* (tomatillo). The green fruit, which often appears in the papery skin of its calyx, is actually a berry and tastes completely different from the tomato. The tomatillo is more acidic in flavor and has an almost gelatinous interior. It's not often eaten alone, but rather diced and added to soups and stews, and, of course, salsas.

Tomatillos are not always available in the East and are easier to find in the southwest and the West where the Mexican population has made them popular. Look for fruit that is firm and evenly colored, and that shows no mold on the calyx.

Guacamole

(Coarse Avocado Salsa)   *Serves 4 to 6*

Some form of Mexican guacamole is a common addition to many Super Bowl buffet tables. All too frequently it's a jarring combination of tastes concocted from a pre-packaged mix. Surrounded by tortilla chips and served with style, nothing compares with the flavor of a real guacamole prepared with the freshest ingredients and served immediately.

3 small firmly ripe Hass avocados, peeled, pitted, and coarsely chopped
1 medium red onion, minced
1 small red bell pepper, seeded and minced
1 small tomato, peeled, seeded, and minced
2 teaspoons minced garlic
3 scallions including 3 inches of the green part, minced
1 tablespoon minced cilantro (optional)
2 teaspoons freshly squeezed lime juice
1 teaspoon Mexican chilli powder
1 teaspoon minced jalapeño chilli, or to taste (see Note, page 120)
Salt and freshly ground black pepper, to taste

Place all of the ingredients into a medium bowl and mix well. Serve immediately with tortilla chips.

Salsa Cruda *Makes about 1 cup*

This is the basic table salsa that comes in almost every Mexican restaurant. I include the recipe here because too many people go out and buy this sauce, which is sinfully easy to prepare.

3 medium, tomatoes, peeled, seeded, and minced
1 small red onion, minced
1 scallion, including 3 inches of the green part, minced
1 tablespoon minced cilantro
1 jalapeño chilli, stemmed, and minced, or to taste (see Note, page 120)
¼ teaspoon minced fresh Mexican oregano (see Note)
Pinch of sugar
Freshly squeezed juice of 1 lime
1 tablespoons olive oil
Salt and freshly ground black pepper, to taste

Mix all of the ingredients together in a non-reactive bowl. Adjust seasonings with salt and pepper, and serve with tortilla chips or slices of jicama.

NOTE: Subsitute fresh Mediterranean oregano if Mexican is not available.

Pico de Gallo   *Makes about 1 cup*

This variant of *salsa cruda* is the Latin American equivalent of ketchup and appears on virtually every home and restaurant table.

3 serrano chillies, stemmed and minced (see Note, page 120)
½ cup minced red onion
1½ tablespoons minced cilantro
Pinch of salt
1 teaspoon freshly squeezed lime juice
2 large tomatoes, peeled seeded, and minced

Mix all of the ingredients together with 2 teaspoons of water in a non-reactive bowl. Serve with grilled meats or tacos.

Roast Corn Salsa   *Makes about 1 cup*

I learned to love the taste of roasted corn in the Caribbean where street vendors sell it on street corners. There's something about the smoky undertaste and the slight hint of char that just takes corn to another level. Next time you're barbecuing, throw another ear or two on the grill, add a couple of jalapeños, and make this salsa.

2 ears corn, roasted
2 roasted jalapeño chillies, peeled, seeded, and minced, or to taste (see Note, page 120)
1 small red onion, minced
½ teaspoon minced garlic
2 tablespoons olive oil
Freshly squeezed juice of 1 lime
1½ tablespoons minced cilantro (optional)
Salt and freshly ground black pepper, to taste

Cut the kernels from the ears of roasted corn and place them in a small non-reactive bowl. Add the jalapeños, onion, garlic, olive oil, lime juice, and cilantro and mix well. Season with salt and pepper. Cover with plastic wrap and refrigerate for at least 3 hours to allow the flavors to mix. Correct the seasoning before serving at room temperature with grilled meats.

Passionfruit-Peach Salsa   *Makes about 2 cups*

This contemporary salsa combines some of my favorite flavors and includes a back note of slightly tart passionfruit that seals the deal.

1½ cups diced, slightly underripe peaches
¼ cup California-style dried apricots, minced
1 small red onion, minced
1 tablespoon minced green bell pepper
2 teaspoons passionfruit nectar
1 tablespoon balsamic vinegar
1 tablespoon freshly squeezed lemon juice
1 tablespoon minced cilantro leaves (optional)
2 jalapeño chillies, seeded and minced, or to taste (see Note, page 120)

Combine all of the ingredients in a non-reactive bowl, mixing well to make sure that the flavors mingle. Cover with plastic wrap and refrigerate for 1 hour. Serve chilled or at room temperature.

Pomegranate Salsa *Serves 4 to 6*

The pomegranate is a marvelous fruit that turns up in the cooking of parts of the Middle East and Mexico. It even gave its name to one of Spain's most famous Moorish cities, Granada. The sweet-tart, ruby-hued seeds add a unique flavor to this salsa which would be equally at home on a table in two very different parts of the world. The trick is in getting the seeds from the pomegranate. It's easier than it looks; try it. First slice the ends off of the pomegranate. Slice the pomegranate skin into quarters, then gently twist the fruit to break it apart. Remove the seeds from each quarter, taking care to discard all of the bitter white membrane.

1 bunch each fresh mint, cilantro, and flat-leaf parsley, chopped
Seeds from 1 pomegranate
1 small onion, minced
¼ cup freshly squeezed lime juice
1 teaspoon grated lime zest
1 jalapeño chilli, stemmed and minced (See Note, page 120)
2 tablespoons extra virgin olive oil

Mix all of the ingredients together in a non-reactive bowl. Cover the salsa with plastic wrap and chill it for 1 hour to allow the flavors to mingle. Serve chilled.

Chapter 4

CHUTNEYS AND RELISHES

As we loll on our verandahs in Gap khakis, or catch the sun in a dinghy off some island where the evening breezes are cool enough to require a shawl, or just relax after yoga with a fruit punch, little do we realize how much we owe to the colonial peregrinations of Europeans. Europe's colonization of Asia, the Americas, Australia, Southeast Asia, Melanesia, and Africa left an imprint that we often forget to acknowledge. In our English language alone, the words verandah, khaki, dinghy, shawl, punch, and, of course yoga, all come from the languages of the Indian subcontinent.

Long before Alexander the Great's voyage to the Indian subcontinent, humankind had been in movement, warring, conquering, and colonizing. As Europe exited the Middle Ages and entered into the world of the Renaissance and the Age of Exploration that followed it, the cuisines of Europe changed. We also tend to forget that during the Middle Ages and in fact up to the voyages of Columbus, much of southern Europe was under the domination of, or living with the residual culture of, the Moorish occupation that lasted for over 700 years. The ebb and flow of foodstuffs and tastes had already begun. Baghdad had been the capital of the Arab world since 763 A.D., thirty-one years after Charles Martel had pushed back the Moors outside of Poitiers, France. The Arab cuisines evidenced tastes for the sweet-and-sour, and these flavors would make their way east to mix with the foods of Mughal India and west to influence the kitchens of Europe.

After the Age of Exploration of the fifteenth and sixteenth centuries, which opened up the map of the world into the format we know today, the desire for trade and then more than trade, ownership, and territorial expansion, resulted in a mixing of cultures that is often unheralded but always fascinating. While Portugal and Spain may have been among the first in the race to establish footholds on the African coast, in Asia, and then in the New World, the Dutch, British, and French weren't far behind. The resulting mixing and merging of cultures over the centuries has changed the life of the world in all ways including the culinary.

The Portuguese reached Malacca in 1509. By 1511, three ships set sail for the Spice Islands and became the first European ships to reach Banda and bring a cargo of nutmegs and cloves back to Europe. The Arab monopolies were broken and the spice wars were on. Europeans, who had already developed a taste for the spicy and used condiments to enhance the flavor of food, not only brought spices back to their northern climes, but also fell in love with the tasty preserved delicacies of India and Southeast Asia during the booming spice trade of the sixteenth and seventeenth centuries. The culinary mixing continued throughout the eighteenth and nineteenth centuries, which were seemingly devoted to Europe's desire to paint the whole world map in shades of British imperial pink and French imperial turquoise.

The British East India Company was founded in 1599 by a group of London merchants who wanted to drive down the cost of pepper. Ships named *Clove, Peppercorn,* and *Trade's Increase* headed off to the South Seas, where the British at first began their wars for nutmeg in Southeast Asia. In 1623, when they were resoundingly defeated by the Dutch for the Spice Islands, they set their sights to the north and moved their interests to the Indian subcontinent. The first British "factory" or entrepot was established at Surat in 1612 and from there they made progressive inroads into the subcontinent. The 1630 Treaty of Madrid granted the British access to Goa in the west for the loading of spices; in 1640 some land was leased in Madras to the south. Bombay was handed over to them in 1668 as a part of the dowry of Catherine of Braganza, and finally, in 1690 Calcutta became home to The British East India Company. By 1757, all was in place for the establishment of the British Raj that would last until January 1, 1947. Other European nations had their days in the colonial sun:

France in Southeast Asia, the Caribbean, and in Central and Western Africa; the Dutch in Southeast Asia, South Africa, and in the Caribbean; and the Portuguese in Africa and Brazil and in smaller outposts like Macao and Goa. However, few European nations gained more culinarily and spread their own colonial tastes around the world as much as the British.

When the British arrived, food in India was changing. The chilli had been introduced by the Portuguese in the sixteenth century along with such other ingredients as pineapples, cashews, and tomatoes, all of which had a major impact on the Indian diet. By 1542, there were three different types of chillies growing on the subcontinent; one of them was named *Pernambuco pepper,* suggesting that the Portuguese may have brought it from that location in northeastern Brazil.

By the end of the seventeenth century, English cooks at home in England were copying the style of the subcontinent, and a 1694 cookery book gives us the first recipe for piccalilli published under the heading "To pickle lila, an Indian pickle." Some think that the word is an elision of pickle and chilli. The British version of this sweet, mustardy relish of mixed vegetables is more chutney-like than its American counterpart. The Crosse and Blackwell label of a commercial version even boasted that it was invented for Napoleon by chef Quailliotti and suggested that when the Corsican emperor was sent into exile on Saint Helena, the chef transferred his allegiance to Crosse and Blackwell in London where his recipe became their master recipe.

Where the British went, so went their piccalilli: on the South Carolina table as *ats jaar* or, as it appears in an 1837 Boston publication cited by food historian William Woys Weaver as Yellow Pickle or Axejar. (The names are a corruption of the Indian term *achar,* meaning pickle.) The mustard-hued relish traveled not only to colonial South Carolina, but also to Southeast Asia and beyond. The Malay have their own *achar* as do the Cape Malay of South Africa. Even the French Caribbean enters into the game with its version of the relish, *achards.*

In South Carolina, *ats jaar* turns up as a condiment traditionally served with country captain, another dish of Indian origin that has followed the colonial route. Just to make things truly complicated, the piccalilli known as *ats jaar* or axejar is often confused with chowchow; indeed, the term seems to be used almost interchangeably. Crosse and Blackwell label their version chowchow in England but call it piccalilli pickle in the U.S. (Incidentally the latter was the product's original name, and comes from the Chinese!)

Piccalilli may have been the earliest recipe to be recorded but the true international travelers of Indian cuisine are the chutneys, not the relishes. For the English, chutney was love at first taste. Chutney comes from the Hindi word *chatni* or *chatnee* meaning a strong, sweet relish. The Hindi word, in turn, comes from an earlier word *chatna* meaning to be licked or tasted. Prepared fresh for meals and sometimes sun-dried and stored for more intense taste, these condiments accompanied the curries and other dishes in the Indian cuisine that would inspire the Anglo-Indian food of the Raj. Today chutneys are distinguished from relishes in that the latter are not cooked, whereas the former are, unless—just to complicate things—they are the original Indian chutneys, which are prepared from raw ingredients. In addition, chutneys or Anglo-Indian chutneys have finely chopped ingredients, and use sweeteners to temper the flavor of the final product.

In the early years of the Raj and throughout the eighteenth century, as the condiments of the colony made their way back to the mother country, British cooks used what they had on hand to mimic the exotic ingredients that might be unavailable. Melons and cucumbers were transformed into "mangoes" by hollowing them out and filling them with a mixture of onions, horseradish, ginger, and spices. In Mrs. Rundell's *A New System of Domestic Cookery,* published in 1806 but undoubtedly containing recipes from the previous century, the author recommends such a switch and suggests that elder shoots take the place of bamboo! These foreign condiments were used mainly in southern England and from there were transported by seafaring folk around the world.

Chutney recipes were more of a family item, likely to be passed down by word of mouth, or simply concocted when there was a bumper crop of fruits and vegetables. They do not appear regularly in English cookbooks until later in the nineteenth century, and Eliza Acton and Mrs. Isabella Beeton, who also have recipes for piccalilli, offer one recipe each for "chetney sauce." Each was said to have originated in India. Acton's uses tomatoes and Beeton's is based on apples and raisins. Neither is cooked.

By Victorian times, the tastes of the Raj became available commercially and brands like Bengal Club and Major Grey's gained the popularity they still enjoy today. Major Grey's brand became so popular that John F. Mackay wrote a brief verse entitled "Rank Injustice" that is quoted by food historian David Burton in *The Raj at Table,* his definitive treatise on the food of Anglo-India:

All things chickeney and mutt'ny
Taste better far when served with chutney
This is the mystery eternal:
Why didn't Major Grey make Colonel?

It's a very good question indeed, as the widely traveled mango chutney immortalized under the good major's name is perhaps the condiment that most characterizes the Raj.

The British Raj, though, is only one facet of the colonial picture. Other nations danced their own versions of the colonial pavane with much the same success—trade first, followed by acquisition of territory. Marco Polo had visited Java in the thirteenth century and Europe had long known the source of the spices that were so coveted. The unstated goal of the Age of Discovery was in fact finding alternate routes to the Indies in order to break the Arab and Venetian monopolies of the spice trade. Although the Portuguese arrived in the Straits of Malacca in 1511, it was the Dutch who eventually gained control over the Spice Islands and reaped enormous profits which allowed them to live in luxury. The United East India Company was incorporated in 1602 and the Dutch controlled the islands until independence in 1949, with a brief interlude of British rule from 1811 to 1816 under the governorship of Thomas Stamford Raffles. In the islands, the Dutch burghers transformed a traditional village feast into the banquet known as a rijsttafel (a term now considered politically incorrect by many as it is a reminder of the humiliations of the colonial experience). The rijsttafel (rice table) was a full-tilt-all-out-gorge with a staggering number of dishes served, each brought to the table and served by a "boy." (Raffles applied the same system to curries in Singapore, resulting in the four-, six-, and ten-boy curries still served there in the hotel that bears his name.) Diners would be presented with two plates: one for the rice and one for the other offerings, which included meats, fish, poultry, and a wide range of condiments known as *sambals.* The *sambals* are chilli- and spice-based relishes designed to go with each of the dishes that add heat to the individual mixtures of dishes. The delicate spicings of the food and indeed many of the *sambals* that accompanied the dishes journeyed with the Dutch, and the Malay whom they enslaved, to the Cape of Good Hope.

When Bartolomeu Dias rounded the Cape of Good Hope in 1488, he was unaware that he'd discovered a sea route to India. Vasco da Gama would circumnavigate Africa in 1497 and saw the province of Natal on Christmas day of that year. Subsequent groups would realize the importance of the Cape. When the Dutch ship *Harlem* broke up off the coast in 1647, two of the shipwrecked crew survived and washed up in Table Bay where they were forced to wait until another ship passed in rescue. When they returned to the Netherlands, they spoke of the bounty of the land that had sustained them and exhorted authorities to establish a settlement on the Cape, insisting that it made a perfect spot for provisioning ships on the India run. Their request was granted and in 1652 Jan van Riebeeck, a ship's surgeon, went ashore with seventy men, building material, agricultural implements, and sacks of seed, and established the Cape Colony.

Soon the colony was so prosperous it became known as the "Tavern of the Two Seas." The Khoi and the San who had originally traded cattle with the passing ships were pressed into servitude and when they proved unwilling, the Dutch brought in enslaved peoples from their Southeast Asian colonies of Java and Malaysia, as well as enslaved Africans from Western Africa and Madagascar all of whom became the laborers of the colony. The lack of European women led to mixed marriages and the heterogeneous mix became the ancestors of the people known today as the Cape Malay or the Cape Muslims. Those who came from Southeast Asia brought with them their culinary knowhow and transformed the traditional Dutch dishes of the settlers with their additions of spices and aromatics and with the multiple condiments of their homelands.

Over the decades, the condiments of Southeast Asia were transformed by culinary proximity with Africans and Europeans into the *sambals* and *blatjangs* and *atjars* of the Cape Malay food of South Africa. By 1891, when Hildagonda J. Duckitt published the first edition of *Hildagonda's How To,* a classic South African colonial cookbook, *sambals* and *blatjangs* had become a part of the country's culinary ethos. C. Louis Leipoldt, whose 1933 *Kos Vir Die Kenne,* printed in English as *Cape Cookery,* is the classic Afrikaaner cookbook, and includes the by-then thoroughly South African condiments in his work as well. The condiments of Southeast Asia thrive, therefore, not only in their native hemisphere but also in South Africa, in the Caribbean where rijsttafel and all of its condiments are still served in an abbreviated and creolized form, and in the Netherlands as well.

The French also had their colonial adventures, and by the end of the nineteenth century governed all of Vietnam, Laos, and Cambodia as well as Tahiti, several of the islands of the Indian Ocean, and large areas of central and western Africa and the Caribbean. Nowhere in the French-speaking world, though, is there more culinary cross-pollination than among the Gallic Départements d'Outre Mer located in the Indian Ocean and the Caribbean Sea. The *rougail* or raw vegetable relish that accompanies the curries of the Île de la Réunion turns up as a condiment in the Caribbean where it is eaten as an appetizer. It even turns up in New Caledonia under the name *roujaire.*

In the English-speaking Caribbean, the chutneys and condiments of the British Raj rejoin the traditional foods of India brought by the indentured servants who replaced enslaved Africans in the third quarter of the nineteenth century. Mango chutney takes on New World flavors as do condiments like the shaved mango relish known as *kuchela,* and numerous other dishes. The immigration of indentured servants from southern India and Sri Lanka to the French-speaking Caribbean has resulted in transplantation of many of their foods. Colombos, the French Antillean versions of curry, take their name from the former capital of Sri Lanka, and their condiments from a variety of places in their formerly colonized native lands. All have undergone a sea change and become something slightly different. The result is another world of chutneys and relishes that range from a classic Caribbean mango chutney that is spicier than its British cousin but milder than its Indian parent, to a chatni that is pounded in a mortar and pestle and includes the New World shadow benny or culantro as one of its ingredients.

A Note about Yields

Yields will vary with time of year and fruit used as there may be more or less liquid. Fill each container to the brim and seal. If you get a bit more, put the extra in your refrigerator for immediate use.

CHUTNEYS AND RELISHES

Singapore Mint Chutney   *Makes about 1¾ cups*

While many of us associate chutney with the spicy, brown jam known as Major Grey's, this chutney takes the idea back to the subcontinent and a traditional mix of fresh green herbs and seasonings. The yogurt cools the dish but there is a definite kick from the chillies, which can be increased to taste. Because of the yogurt, this chutney is almost like an Indian *raita*. It can be thinned a bit further with the addition of a tablespoon or two of water to become an excellent salad dressing for a mix of sturdy greens like iceberg or romaine.

1 cup minced fresh cilantro

¼ teaspoon minced fresh bird chillies, or to taste (See Note, page 120)

2 tablespoons freshly squeezed lemon juice

½ cup minced fresh mint leaves

2 teaspoons minced fresh ginger

¼ teaspoon salt, or to taste

4 tablespoons unflavored yogurt

Place all of the ingredients in the bowl of a food processor and process to a fine slurry. Pour into a small bowl, cover with plastic wrap, and refrigerate for 1 hour. Serve chilled with curries.

Padina *Chatni*   *Serves 4*

This minty chutney is a cross between a chutney and a raita, and is wonderfully cooling with some of the spicier Indian dishes. I also like it served as a snack or a nibble served with crisp pappadams.

⅔ cup unflavored yogurt
2½ cups minced fresh mint leaves
2 hot green bird chillies, seeded and minced, or to taste (see Note page 120)
2 teaspoons freshly squeezed lemon juice
Red pepper flakes for garnish

Place yogurt, mint, chillies, and lemon juice in a small, non-reactive bowl and mix well. Cover with plastic wrap and refrigerate for 1 hour. Remove and check the seasonings. Sprinkle the top with red pepper flakes. Serve chilled.

Traditional Pineapple Chutney   *Serves 6*

This chutney takes the traditional route: it is an uncooked chutney of mixed raw ingredients. The trick is to select a pineapple that is ripe but not too juicy, and that still has a bit of acidity along with the sugar.

1 large firm pineapple
1 medium red onion, minced
½ habanero chilli, seeded and minced, or to taste (see Note, page 120)
4 cloves garlic, minced
1-inch piece ginger, peeled and grated
2 teaspoons sugar, or to taste
3 tablespoons freshly squeezed lime juice, or to taste
Salt and freshly ground black pepper, to taste

Peel the pineapple, core it, and chop it coarsely. Drain the pineapple pieces on paper towels and place them into a non-reactive bowl. Add the onion, chilli, garlic, sugar, and lime juice. Season with salt and pepper. You may want to add more lime juice, sugar, salt, pepper, or, if you're a real chillihead, habanero. Cover with plastic wrap and refrigerate for 1 hour. Serve chilled.

Bernice's Mixed Berry Chutney   *Makes about 2 pints**

I make most of my chutney at my house on Martha's Vineyard. There I take advantage of bumper crops of summer fruits and vegetables at the local farmers' market—so my chutneys are not always prepared with the traditional fruits. One chutney I came up with in a pinch takes advantage of the Vineyard's bounty of berries. I first prepared it for a dinner I took to a friend I called the Empress of Oak Bluffs, nonagenarian Bernice Slaughter. This past summer when I arrived on the Vineyard, I was distressed to hear that she had died before making it back for yet another year. Her daughter, Liz, stopped by and we reminisced and poured some rum for her mother. I made dinner and we celebrated the memory of our mothers with this chutney.

1 cup raspberries, cleaned
1 cup strawberries, cleaned and hulled
5 cups blueberries
1 small piece fresh ginger, peeled and minced
¼ habanero chilli, seeded and minced, or to taste (see Note, page 120)
½ cup cider vinegar
½ cup sugar

Place all of the ingredients in a non-reactive saucepan and bring to a boil. Lower the heat and cook for an hour, stirring occasionally, until the chutney has a jammy texture. (Toward the end you'll have to stir more frequently to make sure it doesn't stick.) Spoon the chutney into sterilized jars. Allow them to cool and then refrigerate them. This chutney doesn't last long enough to need processing, but it you decide to make a larger batch, process accordingly (see page 103).

*See "A Note about Yields" on page 137.

Minted Apricot Chutney   *Makes about 1 pint**

This chutney mixes fresh and dried apricots with a hint of fresh mint. It's another recipe I concocted in my kitchen in Massachusetts.

½ pound fresh apricots, halved, pits removed
½ habanero chilli, or to taste (see Note, page 120)
1-inch piece of ginger, peeled and coarsely chopped
½ cup cider vinegar
½ cup sugar
2 cloves garlic
¼ teaspoon salt
4 sprigs fresh mint, leaves only, chopped
½ cup California dried apricots, cut into ½-inch pieces

Place all of the ingredients except the dried apricots in a food processor and pulse until you have a paste. Spoon the mixture into a non-reactive saucepan and stir in the dried apricot pieces. Bring to a boil over high heat, then lower the heat and simmer, stirring occasionally, for 45 minutes, or until the mixture becomes jammy. Remove it from the heat and spoon it into sterilized jars. Seal and refrigerate.

*See "A Note about Yields" on page 137.

Gail McDonough's Green Mango Chutney *Makes about 6 pints**

This recipe was given to my friend, Gail McDonough, by her friends, Mary and Del Layton, who were legendary in South Florida. Both are dead now but stories are still told. When she knew them best, in the 1970s, they were living on one of the Florida Keys, which they owned. Del proclaimed himself Mayor, Police, and Fire Chief and anything else he could think of. He'd been a fishing and poker-playing pal of Hemingway and Howard Hughes and lived that whole era to the hilt. Mary was a character in her own right with a heart as wide open as her arms. She was a legendary cook and Del kept a stone crab tank for her beside his boat.

5 pounds mature green mangoes, peeled, seeded, and cut into small slices

2 large onions, coarsely chopped

2 green bell peppers, stemmed, seeded, and coarsely chopped

1 cup raisins

1 tablespoon ground cinnamon

1 teaspoon ground cloves

1 teaspoon ground allspice

2 teaspoon salt

4 ounces (about a cup) crystallized ginger, finely chopped

1 cup underripe papaya (1 small, peeled, cut in half, seeded, and cubed)

2 cloves garlic, peeled and chopped

1 key lime, seeded and chopped

3 cups brown sugar

1 quart red wine vinegar

¼ teaspoon cayenne pepper

6 tamarind pods or 3 tablespoons tamarind paste (see Note)

Combine the mangoes, onions, green peppers, raisins, cinnamon, cloves, allspice, salt, ginger, papaya, garlic, lime, brown sugar, vinegar, and cayenne in a large, non-reactive pot. Bring to a boil, lower the heat, and boil gently, stirring occasionally, for fifteen minutes or until the mangoes are fork-tender.

While the chutney is cooking, shell the tamarind pods and soak the seeds and pulp in warm water to cover until the seeds can be removed with ease. Strain the pulp well and discard the seeds. (If using paste, you can omit this.) Add the tamarind pulp or paste to the pot, mix well, and taste. Add more brown sugar, if you like. Boil gently for another hour, stirring often. Spoon into hot sterilized jars and seal.

NOTE: Tamarind is the most important ingredient, after the mangoes, so don't leave it out. See Mail Order Sources, page 199.

*See "A Note about Yields" on page 137.

Summer Tomato Chutney   *Makes about 3 pints**

It's not summer and I'm not on Martha's Vineyard unless I've spent time in the kitchen preparing tomato chutney from the ripe, red, summer-wonderful tomatoes I purchase at Norton's farmstand. Some years I'll use dark raisins, but recently I've enjoyed the look of golden raisins, so they're included in this recipe.

12 large ripe tomatoes, peeled
¼ pound (about a 5-inch piece) ginger, peeled and coarsely chopped
10 cloves garlic
½ habenero chilli, seeded, or to taste
6 medium onions, coarsely chopped
1½ cups sugar
1½ cups cider vinegar
1 cup golden raisins

Place the tomatoes, ginger, garlic, chillis, and onions in the bowl of a food processor and pulse until you have a thick paste. Spoon the paste into a non-reactive saucepan and stir in the sugar, vinegar, and raisins. Bring to a boil, then lower the heat and simmer over very low heat for 45 minutes to 1 hour, stirring occasionally, until the mixture thickens and becomes jammy. Spoon the mixture into canning jars and process (see page 103), or seal and refrigerate. Serve chilled or at room temperature with grilled chicken or other grilled or roasted meats.

*See "A Note about Yields" on page 137.

ON THE SIDE

Relishes

Relishes such as piccalilli in all of its permutations, *sambals,* and *rougails* take their English designation from the Middle English word *reles,* meaning a taste or aftertaste, odor, or scent. The Middle English harks back to the Old French *reles* meaning something left behind. Even today the word can be used as multiple parts of speech ranging from the noun (a condiment) to the verb (taking delight in the condiment) to the adjective (describing the tray on which it is served).

Traditionally, relishes are uncooked condiments prepared from a mix of fruit and seasonings, or fruits and vegetables and seasonings, and include the *sambals* of Southeast Asia and of the Cape Malay, and the *rougails* of the Indian Ocean. Relishes also include the multiple dishes prepared over the years by European cooks covering everything from the classic green tomato one that my mother would make during the summertime, to the great corn relishes of the South, to the pickle relish that is *de rigueur* on American hot dogs. Relishes are traditionally cut into more uniform pieces and are not as jammy in consistency as chutneys. While most of the traditional relishes of Asian cuisines are not cooked, many of the more modern ones are. Finally, some insist that relishes are never preserved in a mustard sauce. Piccalilli, though, puts the lie to that.

A Quirky Glossary of Selected Chutney and Relish Ingredients

Allspice
(Pimenta dioica)

Allspice fooled poor old Columbus. When he spied it growing on trees in Jamaica, he thought it was the pepper he was searching for. The fruit of a tropical evergreen related to the clove tree, allspice, also known as Jamaica pepper, and pimiento, was known to the Aztecs who used it to flavor their chocolate. It was introduced to Europe in the seventeenth century and became widely used in pickling. The English name comes from the fact that the flavor of the aromatic berry resembles a mix of cloves, cinnamon, and nutmeg. Allspice is the major flavoring in Jamaican jerk, and turns up in several chutney recipes as well.

When purchasing allspice, buy whole berries and grind them yourself. When a recipe calls for a certain number of berries, remember that some can be almost peppercorn in size while others are considerably larger. Use your judgment and your tastebuds.

Apples
(Malus pumila)

While apples seem to be as American as the proverbial pie that is made from them, they in fact probably originated in southwestern Asia and are some of the world's oldest fruits. They were found growing wild in prehistoric Europe and were eaten by the Romans who knew of 37 different varieties. The straight Roman roads brought apples to northern Europe, and from England they arrived in the United States. There are over 10,000 varieties of apples with almost 3,000 suitable for commercial use. As apples may be preserved for long periods of time, they were one of the few fruits available to many during the winter months and were often found in the chutneys that were put up after the end of the harvest season.

Purchasing apples is a matter of taste. The French prefer Golden Delicious apples; the British favor aromatic ones like Cox's Orange Pippin; Americans go for ripe Red Delicious; and the Australian Granny Smith is gaining worldwide currency for its crisp tartness.

When purchasing apples for chutneys, select apples that are firm and without blemishes. The

Gala, Idared, Granny Smith, and McIntosh varieties are my favorites for cooking, but find the ones that best suit your tastes. Remember, though, for chutneys, you're better off with a slightly underripe apple that is acidic, juicy, and high in pectin.

Apricots
(Prunus armeniaca)

Apricots grow wild in parts of China and Japan, and it is now thought that they originated there. It is believed that Alexander the Great may have brought the fruit from Asia to Armenia where earlier folks thought that it originated, hence the Latin name. The sweet-tart fruit is much prized in the cuisines of the eastern Mediterranean and the English word apricot is a corruption of the Spanish-Arab term *al barquq* meaning precious.

Apricots are seasonally available and should be handled with care as they bruise and spoil when damaged.

Dried apricots are available all year round. You may select the Turkish type or the more acidic California type, preserved with sulfur dioxide. Dried apricots, too, can be used in chutneys and relishes, and make an interesting taste and texture contrast to the fresh fruit.

Bananas
(Musa sapientium)

While many believe that the apple was the forbidden fruit of the Bible, others opt for the banana. The plant, actually a giant herb of the orchid family, is thought to have originated in Malaysia and is nearly a million years old. Bananas were brought to Northern Africa about 700 A.D. by the Arabs, and made it to the Western coast of Africa by the fifteenth century. From there, Brazil and the West Indies were next on the fruit's international journey. Bananas found good homes in the New World and today the term "banana republic" is a testimonial, albeit pejorative, to their former economic importance in Central America.

Bananas are available year-round and for making a chutney or relish should be selected when slightly firm to the touch.

Carrots

(see page 46)

Cardamom

(Elettaria cardamomum and

Cardamom is the world's third most expensive spice after saffron and vanilla, and is a member of the ginger family. Known to the Greeks and the Romans, who used it for medicinal purposes, cardamom is popular today in the cooking of India and the Middle East, where it is also used to flavor coffee. Surprisingly, the spice is also popular in the food of Scandinavia where it is used in mulled wines, preserved meats, baked goods, and fruit compotes.

Cardamom is available in pod form, as whole seeds, and ground. It is preferable to purchase the pods and remove the seeds as needed. Two varieties are available: green and white.

Cinnamon

(Cinnamomum zelanicun and cinnamomum cassia)

The tree, a relative of the bay laurel and the avocado, has a bark that is processed into one of the world's oldest aromatic spices. Cinnamon (as cassia) was known to the ancient Chinese and is mentioned in an early botanical treatise that dates back to 2500 B.C. It was one of the plants used by the Egyptians and is mentioned in the Christian Bible. The tree is thought to be a native of Sri Lanka.

If you're used to the powdered cinnamon that your mother used to make cinnamon toast, prepare yourself for a surprise. True cinnamon, not to be confused with cassia or Chinese cinnamon that is a less expensive substitute, is wonderfully warm and aromatic. Purchase it by sticks or quills a few at a time as the spice will not retain its pungency indefinitely. It's readily available.

Cloves

(Syzgium aromaticum)

These are the dried unopened flower buds of an evergreen plant related to myrtle. The spice has been used for over 2,000 years and was originally used in China for perfuming the breath when speaking to the emperor. Marco Polo mentioned seeing clove plantations in the Spice Islands in the thirteenth century. The Portuguese discovered the Moluccas in the sixteenth century and began a spice monopoly, but they were displaced by the Dutch a century later. The Dutch restricted the growth of the tree to the island of Amboina in order to keep the price of cloves up. The French managed to break the monopoly and began the cultivation of the plants in Mauritius in 1770. From there, seedlings were conveyed to Zanzibar, where they thrived. That island today is the center of the world's largest production of the spice.

Each tree yields about 100 pounds of flowers annually with the cloves defined by their place of origin: those from Penang are the most prized, those of Zanzibar follow second, and those from Madagascar come third in value. The English word clove is a corruption of the Latin *clavus* meaning nail.

As with other spices, cloves are best purchased in small quantities and whole. Ground cloves lose their flavor very quickly.

Coriander Seeds

Coriandrum sativum)

These are seeds of the plant that is also known as cilantro or Chinese parsley. (See also Cilantro, page 120.)

Cumin

(Cuminum cyminum)

The cumin plant is related to dill, caraway, and fennel. The plant is native to Upper Egypt and the Mediterranean region, and it has been cultivated in those regions for thousands of years. Ancient Egyptians used it in embalming, and it was known to the ancient Romans. In medieval Europe it was thought that cumin strengthened lovers' fidelity. Cumin is mentioned in the Bible in Matthew 23:23, where the Pharisees are criticized for carefully paying their tithe of mint, anise, and cumin while forgetting about more important matters of the law.

As with all spices, it is better to purchase whole cumin seeds in small quantities and grind them as needed.

Garlic

(see page 47)

Ginger

(Zingiber officinale)

Ginger seems to have been used as a spice and a medicine by both the Chinese and the Indians, as there are references to it in both early Chinese and Sanskrit literature. It was widely used in Asia for its alleged aphrodisiac properties and is featured as such in one of the stories of *The Thousand and One Nights.* The Romans used it mainly for medicinal purposes and thought that it came from Arabia. The rhizome appears to have reached France and Germany in the ninth century and England a bit later. The Spaniards brought it to the New World early on and it was being cultivated for export from Jamaica as early as 1547.

Ginger is available fresh, dried, preserved, and powdered. If you're buying fresh ginger, look for firm rhizomes that are free of wrinkles and free of mold. It will store in the refrigerator for several weeks and can be frozen without losing much of its taste, but it will change texture and soften. If using powdered ginger, buy small quantities and store it in an airtight container.

Mangoes

(Mangifera indica)

The chutney ingredient par excellence is the mango. It's sometimes called the bathtub fruit by connoisseurs who believe the best way to consume a ripe one is naked in the tub. A fresh mango is a relatively recent delight for many, as mangoes were only able to travel with the invention of refrigeration. The British were familiar with the fruit—which has been cultivated in India for more than 6,000 years—because of their colonizing efforts on the Indian subcontinent. Mangoes originated in India but by the first century A.D. had begun to spread eastwards to China, and by the tenth century had spread as far as Persia. The Portuguese brought mangoes to Africa in the sixteenth century and to Brazil in the eighteenth. The fruit arrived in the Caribbean in the eighteenth century as well, but it took until the nineteenth century for it to make its way to Florida, Hawaii, and Mexico.

Today, the mango has almost become an international symbol of the tropics and is symbolic of home to many who hark from countries where mangoes have long been a part of the diet. There are over 1,000 varieties of mangoes. Almost no tropical childhood coming-of-age story is complete without a scene of stealing mangoes from a neighbor's tree, coupled in most cases with a tummyache from eating too many green ones.

When purchasing mangoes, look for heavy fruit that yields slightly to the touch. Color depends on variety, but all unripe mangoes are green.

Nutmeg

(Myristica fragrans)

Native to the Banda Islands, nutmeg was probably not known to the ancient world. They appear in Europe only in the twelfth century. When the Dutch gained control of the Spice Islands at the beginning of the seventeenth century, they began a monopoly on trade of nutmeg that they maintained for 150 years until it was broken by the French, who obtained seedlings and planted the trees in Mauritius. In 1796, Christopher Smith went to the Moluccas on behalf of the East India Company, also obtained seedlings, and planted them in Penang where the spice has been produced since 1802. Nutmeg would later arrive in the Caribbean where it still thrives in Grenada, perfuming the air with its distinctive scent.

Two spices are obtained from the nutmeg tree: nutmeg, the kernel of the nutmeg fruit, and mace, the lacy red aril (membrane-like covering of the nut). If you've never experienced freshly grated nutmeg, purchase a grater and some nuts and treat yourself. Remember, many of the nutmegs that are sold need to be shelled before grating, so give it a good crack, remove the nutmeg from the shell, then grate away and enjoy.

Pineapple

(Ananas comosus)

While most of the ingredients used in chutneys and Asian relishes traveled from the East to the West, the pineapple made the journey in the opposite direction. This bromeliad is thought to have originated in Brazil where similar plants grow wild; the plant has been cultivated in South America and the Caribbean for centuries. Columbus saw pineapple in 1493 in Guadeloupe and loved it. Spanish sailors brought the pineapple to Europe and horticulturalists managed to grow it. The Portuguese brought the fruit from Brazil to much of the rest of the world, which explains why in other languages the fruit's name is a variant of the Tupi word *nana* or *anana* (except that the Brazilians themselves call it *abacaxi* in Bahia). We get our word pineapple from the Spanish *piña,* so dubbed by the sailors for its resemblance to the pinecone.

Pineapples were being grown in India and in parts of Southeast Asia by 1583, and the British brought it to Hawaii in 1790. During the seventeenth and eighteenth centuries in Europe, pineapples became a decorative motif, appearing on everything from door lintels and gate posts to intricately carved four-poster beds. The fruit became the symbol of hospitality and is seen as such on entranceways throughout the English-speaking former colonial world of North America and the Caribbean.

Pineapples are readily available. Ripe pineapples should be heavy and aromatic, and a leaf should pull easily from the thorny crown at the top. Pineapples are very perishable and bruise easily, so they should be purchased as needed.

Raisins

(Vitis spp.)

Raisins are the dried fruit of one of the world's oldest plants, the grape. Grapes may have been cultivated in western Asia over 7,000 years ago. Some palentologists suggest that *Homo habilis,* a forerunner of *Homo erectus,* may have been acquainted with wild grapes as much as 2 million years ago. The Phoenicians brought the art of grape cultivation to much of the Mediterranean basin along with the art of wine-making.

Columbus brought European vines to the New World in 1493 and by the 1530s there were vineyards planted outside of Lima, Peru. Allowing grapes to dry and become raisins to assure a supply of fruit in the off-season is a practice almost as old as the cultivation of grapes itself. Raisins have long been an ingredient in many chutneys both in England and the Caribbean.

Raisins are readily available. When selecting raisins for chutneys, think: do you want a lighter or darker color? Some folks plump them, before use but I think it's unnecessary as they plump while cooking.

Sugar Cane
(Sacharum officinarum)

Whether a tip of sugar in a fresh relish to take down the acidity of the fruit, or a cupful in a chutney to help bring out the flavors and act as a preservative, the flavorful sap of the "honey-bearing reed" is a must for making chutneys or relishes. Even before sugar became the common currency it is today, chutneys were sweetened with molasses, honey, or palm sugar. Sugar cane, a native of the South Seas, came early to India and was first processed into granulated sugar there during the Harappan period of the Indus Valley, 3200 to 2000 B.C. It was noticed by Alexander the Great and thus began its conquest of the culinary world. By the seventh century A.D., it had reached the shores of the eastern Mediterranean and in 1493 Columbus brought it to the New World from the Canary Islands on his second voyage.

The plant grew and thrived but it took the Dutch perfecting the plantation system in Pernambuco, Brazil, for it to become a viable money-making crop. Then, in the seventeenth century, the Sugar Revolution changed the face of the Caribbean and other areas of the Western Hemisphere socially, politically, agriculturally, and economically. Small land holdings became outmoded as sugar could only be grown economically on large estates. The arduous task of growing the cane and processing it into sugar, molasses, and rum, a valuable by-product, was the labor of the hundreds of thousands of slaves imported from Africa. Cane created the glory days of the West Indies when the phrase "as rich as a West Indian planter" indicated great wealth and was heard in the fanciest salons of Great Britain.

Up until recently, we have been removed from the true taste of sugar, seeing the refined white crystals instead of the intense-tasting real thing. A push to natural foods has shown us that unrefined sugar is better for us. Many people will opt for the cane taste of muscovado sugar, which is the last sugar in the barrel after the molasses has been drained off. Brown sugar and the darker black sugar are still available in the Caribbean—a treat for those who get to cook with them. Demerara sugar is a dry, coarse-textured raw sugar from Guyana. The type of sugar you select will affect the final look and taste of your chutney. With the naturally processed sugars of the Caribbean, you will add a hint of a molasses undertone, as well as a darker hue, to the final chutney.

Trinidadian Mango *Kuchela*   *Makes about 2 cups*

I had my first taste of *kuchela* over 25 years ago in a friend's home in Trinidad. It was love at first bite. I remember carefully carrying home a precious cargo of two jars prepared by her Granny, which I husbanded for years until prudence dictated that they be finished or discarded. It took me more than a decade to find the condiment again, but I did in a supermarket in Barbados, where Trinidad's culinary influence is evident on the spice shelves. After reading the ingredient list and remembering the taste of Granny's, I began to experiment and came up with this one. It's not Granny's, but it will more than do. Try it with curried dishes, or as a condiment with roasted meats. Please note that *kuchela* can only be prepared from green mangoes; it cannot be made from ripe ones.

2 cups grated green mango flesh (about three medium mangoes, peeled)
5 cloves garlic, minced
1 habanero chilli, seeded and minced, or to taste (see Note, page 120)
2 teaspoons garam masala (see Note)
2 tablespoons mustard oil (see Note)
4 tablespoons vegetable oil (approximately)

Preheat the oven to 250 degrees. Wrap the mango flesh in a piece of cheesecloth and squeeze as much liquid from it as possible. Discard the liquid or save it for another use. Spread the mango pulp on a baking sheet and bake it in the oven for about 2 hours, or until it is completely dried. Combine the mango pulp, garlic, habanero, garam masala, and mustard oil in a bowl and mix well. Add only enough vegetable oil to make a thick sauce. Pour into sterilized jars, close the tops, and store in the refrigerator. The *kuchela* will keep in the refrigerator for 2 weeks, or it can be processed for longer preservation.

NOTE: See Mail Order Sources, page 199.

Ats Jaar *Makes about 6 quarts*

My friend John Martin Taylor, whom I call "Bubba," and whom the world knows as Hoppin' John, has written *the* book on the cooking of the Lowcountry: *Hoppin' John's Lowcountry Cooking*. He used to have a wondrous cookbook store in Charleston where, for a while, I held the record for buying the most cookbooks in one spending spree. He's closed the store, but he has a great online boutique where he sells items like magnificent stone-ground grits and wonderful Lowcountry condiments. When I asked him for a recipe for one of his favorites, he responded with this one for *Ats Jaar*, the Lowcountry take on the *achars* of India, and reminded me that "mixed pickles in the Indian manner have graced Lowcountry tables for centuries." You'll make about 6 quarts of pickles. If you only want a few quarts, log on to *www.Hoppinjohns.com* and order a jar or two of John's very own.

For the vegetables:
1 cup sea salt
1 gallon cold water
½ pound fresh young string beans, topped and tailed
1 pound (about ½ head) green cabbage, cut into small pieces
1½ pounds small cucumbers, peeled and cut into 1-inch slices
2 pounds (1 head) cauliflower, broken into small florets
12 carrots, peeled and cut into 2-inch pieces
1 pound (about 7 ribs) celery, cut into 2-inch pieces
½ pound radishes, cut into ½-inch dice
1 pound (about 8 small) onions, peeled and halved or left whole if very small
½ pound (about 5 heads) garlic separated into cloves and peeled

For the pickling solution:

¼ pound (about a 5-inch piece) ginger, peeled and thinly sliced

1 tablespoon ground turmeric

3 tablespoons whole mustard seeds

3 or 4 fresh or pickled chilli peppers (1 for every other jar)

½ gallon distilled white vinegar

To prepare the vegetables, dissolve the salt in the water, then pour over the prepared vegetables in a non-reactive container. Let stand overnight, at least 12 hours.

The next day, combine the ginger, turmeric, mustard seeds, chillies, and vinegar in a large, non-reactive pot. Drain the vegetables well and pack them into hot, sterile jars. Bring the pickling solution to a boil, then pour it over the vegetables to ¼ inch from the top of the jars. Seal and process in a boiling water bath for 10 minutes or refrigerate for a few days before eating.

Achards, Martinique-style   *Serves 4 to 6*

This Martinique version of *achards* retains the golden color of the Charleston version thanks to the addition of a bit of saffron, but it doesn't have the mustardy bite. It is usually served as a chilled condiment salad at the beginning of the meal.

ON THE SIDE

1 pound vegetables, including hearts of palm, cabbage, cauliflower, carrots, and string beans
Sea salt
¼ cup olive oil
1 medium onion, thinly sliced
1 clove garlic, minced
½ habanero chilli, or to taste, seeded and minced (see Note, page 120)
2 or 3 pinches saffron threads

Wash and trim the vegetables and cut them into bite-sized pieces. Place each vegetable in a separate container of lightly salted water and chill them for 24 hours.

The next day, heat the oil and sauté the onion, garlic, chilli, and saffron until the onion is golden. Meanwhile, remove the vegetables from the refrigerator, drain them well, and arrange them on a serving platter. Pour the hot oil over the vegetables and mix it in well. Cover with plastic wrap and refrigerate overnight. Serve chilled.

Tomato Relish   *Makes six 8-ounce canning jars**

There are many varieties of tomato relish. This one from New Zealand cooks the ingredients to produce a cross between a chutney and a mustard pickle. It also uses corn flour to thicken the relish, as was done in the old days. The recipe comes from the mother of my friend, Robert Oliver, a New York–based chef.

12 large tomatoes, peeled, seeded, and coarsely chopped
6 onions, minced
1 pound (2¼ cups) sugar
2 cups apple cider vinegar
1 tablespoon sea salt
1½ teaspoon dry mustard powder or prepared English mustard
1½ teaspoon curry powder
1 tablespoon corn flour

Place the tomatoes, onions, sugar, vinegar, salt, mustard, and curry powder in a large non-reactive saucepan and bring to a boil. Lower the heat and simmer for about 1 hour, or until the mixture thickens. Mix the corn flour with enough water to make a slurry, and stir it into the relish. Cook only until the mixture is thickened and clear. Allow to cool slightly. Pour the relish into sterilized jars, cap, and keep in the refrigerator for a few weeks before use.

*See "A Note about Yields" on page 137.

Mommy's Green Tomato Relish   *Makes about 4 pints**

It's always a case of "do what I say, don't do what I do" with most folks, and I'm just like the rest of them. Although I learned to cook in my mother's kitchen under her watchful eye, and cooked with her for more than 53 years, I didn't get all of the recipes. Somehow I just never thought she'd die, so I'm thrilled when every now and then I open one of her cookbooks and find a favorite recipe annotated to her own specifications; in this way I am able to reclaim another of Mom's recipes. This recipe for green tomato relish is a favorite find. She'd make it in the summertime when she could get her hands on plenty of unripe, green tomatoes.

12 medium green tomatoes
1 scant tablespoon sea salt
1 cup minced onion
½ cup minced green bell pepper
1 cup minced red bell pepper
½ cup sugar
1 cup cider vinegar
2 tablespoons whole pickling spices
  (often available on grocery spice racks)

Chop the tomatoes and place them in a non-reactive bowl. Add the salt and let the mixture stand overnight, covered, at room temperature. The next day drain off the liquid and add the onion, green and red pepper, sugar, and vinegar, and mix well. Pour the mixture into a non-reactive saucepan. Place the pickling spices in a small piece of cheesecloth, tie it securely, and place it in the mixture. Bring it to a boil, lower the heat, and allow it to simmer for 1½ hours. Remove the spice bag and spoon the relish into sterilized jars. Process or refrigerate.

*See "A Note about Yields" on page 137.

Corn Relish   *Makes about 2½ pints*

I've always been partial to corn relish. I had my first taste decades ago at a restaurant called Munroe's Boston House in Oak Bluffs on Martha's Vineyard and it was love at first bite. The mix of sweet and tart and the colorful flecks of minced bell pepper will always mean summer to me. It is one of the relishes that I search out whenever possible. This recipe is one of myriad variations on the subject. If you don't want to make your own or if you're stuck with old ears of corn in the winter, go to the web and order some from my friend Hoppin' John Taylor (see page 160). His corn relish tastes just like Munroe's to me.

5 cups fresh corn, cut from the cob (about 10 ears)
1 cup minced onion
1 cup minced green bell pepper
1 cup minced red bell pepper
½ cup sugar
2 teaspoons salt
2 teaspoons celery seed
1 teaspoon prepared dry English mustard
  or powdered dry mustard
1 teaspoon mustard seed
1½ cups cider vinegar

Place all the ingredients in a non-reactive saucepan and bring to a boil. Cover, lower the heat, and simmer for 15 minutes, stirring occasionally to make sure the ingredients do not stick. Spoon the relish into sterilized jars and process (see page 103), or refrigerate and eat within 2 weeks. Serve with grilled chicken, eat it out of the jar, or serve it with almost anything.

Onion Relish   *Makes about 1 cup*

There are many variations on this onion and chilli relish served in India, where it accompanies tandoori dishes. This one is super hot, and simple to make.

3 medium onions, diced
1 serrano chilli, seeded and minced, or to taste (see Note, page 120)
1 teaspoon red pepper flakes, or to taste
2 teaspoons freshly squeezed lemon juice
Salt, to taste

Place the onions, chilli, pepper flakes, and lemon juice in a non-reactive bowl and mix well. Salt to taste and mix again. Serve at room temperature.

Onion Salad Relish   *Serves 6 to 8*

This recipe was given to my buddy Gail McDonough in New Orleans by her friend, Stephanie Musser. The great thing about these onions is that they can be served as a salad, used as a relish with meats, or eaten on crackers as an hors d'oeuvre. They also make an innovative addition to any egg, tuna, or chicken salad. The recipe is in this chapter because the onions are so versatile and also because of their hint of mustard.

4 large sweet onions (Vidalia, Texas Sweets, or Maui), diced
1 cup sugar
1½ cups distilled white vinegar
¼ teaspoon dry mustard powder
1 cup good-quality mayonnaise (Hellman's always worked for my mother)
¼ teaspoon celery seed
¼ teaspoon freshly ground black pepper

Spread the onions in a 9 x 13-inch Pyrex baking dish. Combine the sugar, vinegar, mustard, and 2 cups of water in a non-reactive saucepan and bring to a boil. Cool the liquid slightly and pour over the onions. Cover the pan with plastic wrap and refrigerate overnight.

The next day, drain the onions. Combine the mayonnaise, celery seed, and black pepper, pour it over the onions, and mix well. Place the onions in sterilized glass jars, cover, and refrigerate. They will keep for up to 3 weeks (if they last that long).

Mango *Chaat*   *Serves 4*

A *chaat* is a mixture of vegetables traditionally served with an Indian meal. In this mix of mango and onions, the extra zing comes from the addition of powered mango known as *amchoor*. Some people add more peanuts, but I only like so much crunch with my food.

2 teaspoons whole cumin seeds

½ teaspoon red pepper flakes, or to taste

1 teaspoon *amchoor* (see Note)

½ teaspoon garam masala (see Note)

Pinch asafetida (optional) (see Note)

1 tablespoon peanut oil

¾ cup unsalted peanuts

1 small red onion, minced

⅓ cup minced cucumber, peeled and seeded

1 firm ripe mango, peeled, pitted, and cut into ½-inch dice

2 green bird chillies, minced, or to taste (see Note, page 120)

1½ tablespoons minced cilantro

1 tablespoon minced fresh mint leaves

1 tablespoon freshly squeezed lime juice

Pinch of light brown sugar

Salt and freshly ground black pepper

Prepare the *chaat masala* (spice mix) by toasting the cumin seed in a dry skillet for a few minutes, then pulverizing them in a spice grinder with the pepper flakes, *amchoor*, garam masala, and asafetida. Place the oil in the same skillet, add the peanuts, and fry them until they are lightly browned. Mix the onion, cucumber, mango, chillies, cilantro, mint, lime juice, and sugar together in a non-reactive bowl and add 1 teaspoon of the *chaat masala*. Adjust the seasonings with salt and pepper to taste, cover with plastic wrap, refrigerate, and let the *chaat* sit for half an hour for the flavors to mix. When ready, spoon the *chaat* into a serving dish and top with an additional teaspoon of the *chaat masala*. Serve slightly chilled or at room temperature.

NOTE: *Chaat masala* will keep for a month in a sealed jar.

See Mail Order Sources, page 199.

Pineapple *Chaat*   *Serves 4 to 6*

This *chaat* is much simpler then the mango *chaat,* and is great for those who prefer their condiments without nuts. The sour flavor comes from tamarind paste, which is easily obtained from one of the Mail Order Sources on page 199.

1 to 2 tablespoons tamarind paste (see Note)
1 ripe medium pineapple, peeled, cored, and cut into ½-inch dice
1 tablespoons minced cilantro, or to taste
Salt, to taste

Spoon the tamarind paste over the pineapple pieces, add the cilantro, and mix well. Add salt to taste and mix again. Cover with plastic wrap and refrigerate for 1 hour. Serve chilled.

NOTE: See Mail Order Sources, page 199.

Sambal Iris   *Serves 4 to 6*

Sambals are the signature condiments of Southeast Asia. Some of the more complex ones build the flavors with ingredients like shrimp paste and tamarind leaves. This follows the K.I.S.S. theory (keep it simple, stupid) and uses only the basics. It goes great with grilled meat, fish, and poultry, and, if you like things hot, with just about everything.

1 medium onion, cut into thin slices
1 small tomato, peeled, seeded, and cut into ¼-inch dice
1 small hot red chilli, seeded and cut into thin julienne (see Note, page 120)
1 small hot green chilli, seeded and cut into thin julienne
¼ cup freshly squeezed lime juice
Pinch of grated lime zest

Combine all of the ingredients in a non-reactive bowl, cover with plastic wrap, and let sit at room temperature for 1 hour. Serve at room temperature.

Rougail de Tomates   *Serves 4 to 6*

On the islands of the Indian Ocean, the role played by *sambals* in Southeast Asia and chutneys and *chaats* in India is taken over by *rougails*. *Rougails*, however, sometimes become dishes in themselves when shrimp, sausages, or other meats are added to them. This is a basic tomato *rougail* from l'Île de la Réunion.

3 ripe medium tomatoes, peeled, seeded and coarsely chopped
1 small red onion, minced
2 small hot green chillies, seeded and minced, or to taste (see Note, page 120)
1 tablespoon minced flat-leaf parsley
2 tablespoons sunflower seed oil
Salt and freshly ground black pepper, to taste

Place all of the ingredients in a non-reactive bowl and mix well. Cover with plastic wrap and allow the *rougail* to sit for 1 hour. Serve at room temperature.

Wortel Sambal *Serves 6*

Like so many other condiments, *sambals* have traveled far afield from their Southeast Asian home. This carrot *sambal* was no doubt brought by the Cape Malay to South Africa, where it accompanies barbecues and curries.

1 pound carrots, peeled and trimmed
2 green cardamom pods
1 dried hot chilli, to taste
1 tablespoon minced fresh ginger
1 teaspoon sea salt
1½ cups sugar
¾ cup distilled white vinegar

Grate the carrots on the large holes of a hand grater or by putting them through the medium grater blade of a food processor. Remove all of the seeds from the cardamom pods and grind the seeds into powder in a spice mill along with the dried chilli. Place the carrots, spice mixture, ginger, salt, sugar, and ½ cup of water in a 3-quart non-reactive saucepan and bring to a boil. Cook, stirring occasionally, for 30 minutes. Add the vinegar, lower the heat, and cook for an additional 30 minutes or until thick, stirring occasionally to make sure that the mixture does not stick to the saucepan. When the *sambal* has thickened, spoon it into a bowl. Cover the bowl with plastic wrap and refrigerate for at least 1 hour. Serve chilled.

Chapter 5

SAVORY SAUCES AND OTHER ENHANCERS

There are chutneys and relishes and pickles galore, but for those of us in the African-Atlantic world the condiment *par excellence* is hot sauce. Hot condiments are legion on both sides of the African-Atlantic. Often, hot sauces seem to be an emblematic ingredient of the way we eat. Though we like our food spicy and hot from chillies and other ingredients, our attention to matters of hospitality means we realize that not everyone may like it as hot as we do. For this reason we offer the option of ratcheting up the heat intensity even further, with a dash of this and a dollop of that. Hence, the hot sauce. There's a wondrous range of them; the long, thin bottles of hot sauce that grace the tables of the American South are only the beginning.

Our way with hot sauce begins most likely in Western Africa, with the lone chilli that sits on a saucer next to the plate of the man of the house. It's minced into a personalized mix and offered to all who'd like an added bit of heat in their meal. The *pili pili* sauces of the continent follow suit and accompany every dish. Some are simple slurries of minced chilli with a dash of lemon juice. Other hot sauces are more complex and may contain vinegar and ginger as well. They're used in continent-wide generality south of the Sahara and are a characteristic of Western and Central African cooking. The taste for the heat crosses the Atlantic and turns up in the cuisines of the African Diaspora. It can be found in the *malagueta* chillies of Brazil: tiny red and green peppers preserved in vinegar or *cachaça* and served with dishes not only in Bahia, but also in Sao Luis de Maranhão, Espiritu Santo, and virtually all over the country. Preserved *pimenta malagueta* can be purchased in bottles at any shop, but is also be prepared at home, where cooks vie for the most potent recipe. I've learned to go lightly until I know just how pungent the sauce is that accompanies my *feijoada* or *moqueca*.

The Caribbean is home to myriad pepper sauces, which is only natural considering that Columbus and later explorers found the Arawaks and Caribes already consuming the sauces when they arrived. Caribbean pepper sauces, which have become a thriving cottage industry in several places, tend to be on the high end of the incendiary scales. This is only logical in an area where Scotch Bonnet chillies and others with names like *Bonda à Man Jacques* (Madame Jacques's Backside), *wiri wiri*, and goat pepper are common currency in the markets. Cooks prepare sauces with names like *Sauce Chien* in Guadeloupe and *Sauce 'Ti Malice* in Haiti, as well as a seemingly infinite round of home-made delicacies designed to blow the roof off of your mouth. Then there are the bottled sauces that are available in supermarkets. Bello's from is a dose of red liquid fire, while Matouk's from Trinidad comes in several strengths as well as in several flavors, the turmeric-hued one is the best known. Even Bermuda, which isn't the Caribbean at all but a linchpin between that region and the United States, offers Outerbridge's stately sherry peppers, a dash of heat that is traditional with the island's fish chowder.

In the United States, in the South, the ghettoes of the North, and wherever African-Americans live and eat, sauces with names like Red Devil, Louisiana Red, and Crystal grace the tables. Tabasco is just fine for Bloody Marys but not for the serious work of table service unless it's a truly upscale establishment. The traditional long, thin bottle is a hallmark of authenticity in our world of condiments. In some places, folks still put up their own chillies in vinegar and serve them up proudly next to the fried chicken and smothered pork chops. In most African-American households hot sauce is the third-member of the condiment quartet that includes ketchup, salt, and pepper. Even before the current vogue for hot sauces made proud chilliheads of Americans of all hues, hot sauces were a major part of our world.

SAVORY SAUCES AND OTHER ENHANCERS

Sauce 'Ti-Malice *Makes about 1 cup*

Bouki and 'Ti-Malice are two main characters in Haitian folktales, and naïve Bouki is constantly the butt of 'Ti-Malice's jokes. Both of them love grilled meat. 'Ti-Malice diligently cooks his for lunch daily, while Bouki simply appears and eats what 'Ti-Malice has prepared, never offering to bring any of his own. Although fond of Bouki, 'Ti-Malice finally decides that he's had enough of the freeloader and prepares a sauce to cure Bouki of his bad habit. He prepares a fiery hot sauce of chillies and slathers it all over the grilled meat for that day's meal. Much to 'Ti-Malice's amazement, Bouki eats even more of the meat than usual. In fact, he's so enamored of the hot sauce, that he runs through town yelling, *"Me zammi, vini goute sauce 'Ti-Malice fe pou Bouki!"* (My friends, come and taste the sauce that 'Ti-Malice has made for Bouki!) *Sauce 'Ti-Malice* accompanies *griots de porc*, a traditional Haitian dish, and other grilled meats in that country. It's a perfect addition to any table for those who like it hot.

2 large onions, minced
2 shallots, peeled and minced
6 tablespoons freshly squeezed lime juice
2 cloves garlic, minced
1 small habanero chilli, stemmed and minced, or to taste (see Note, page 120)
Salt and freshly ground black pepper, to taste
3 tablespoons olive oil

Mix the onions and shallots with the lime juice in a non-reactive bowl and allow them to marinate for 1 hour at room temperature. Pour the mixture into a small, non-reactive saucepan and add the garlic, chilli, salt and pepper, and oil. Bring to a boil over medium heat, stirring occasionally. Lower the heat. Cook for 10 minutes. Remove from the heat and let cool. Serve with grilled meats and regale your friends with the tale of 'Ti-Malice and Bouki.

Patricia's *Chimichurri* *Makes approximately ½ cup*

One recent summer my buddy Patricia Wilson came to visit me on Martha's Vineyard. As only one of my foodie friends would dare, she arrived with nothing but a cooler full of goodies and treats. She even brought a vat of her own special *chimichurri* for us to savor over a London broil we'd seasoned up and slapped on the grill. A chef/instructor at Johnson and Wales in Miami, Patricia specializes in the cooking of the Americas, notably Puerto Rico. She makes the *chimichurri* by the vat-full because, as she puts it, "it keeps well, and travels with me to top boiled or broiled lobster, fish, steak, pork, or to mix into seafood stews and soups." What more need be said?

1 head garlic, peeled and separated into cloves
Salt
1 bunch flat-leaf parsley, leaves only
¼ cup fresh oregano leaves, chopped
1 teaspoon red pepper flakes, or to taste
Extra virgin olive oil
Freshly squeezed juice of one lemon
Pepper, to taste

In a mortar and pestle, mash the garlic with a sprinkling of salt. (You can do this in a food processor but the texture won't be the same.) Place the garlic in a small bowl, add the parsley leaves, and mix them with the oregano and red pepper flakes. Add enough olive oil to make a paste. Add the lemon juice, mix well, and season to taste with salt and pepper. Serve with just about everything.

Scotch Bonnet Pepper Sauce   *Makes about 2 pints**

Gail McDonough, my official "big sistah," lives in New Orleans where she and her husband, Birch, take me on eating forays to wonderful restaurants. She grew up in Jamaica, a country she deeply loves, and occasionally delights me with tales of growing up there in the 1940s and '50s. Her mother received this recipe for pepper sauce in the early forties from a Mrs. MacCauley, one of the *grandes dames* of old Jamaican families. Gail remembers it fondly from her childhood and offered it up when we were discussing hot sauces.

8 Scotch Bonnet chillies, stemmed (see Note, page 120)
2½ pounds ripe tomatoes, chopped
1 large onion
¾ cup brine (see Note)
½ cup distilled white vinegar
5 whole allspice berries
2 heaping tablespoons butter

Place the Scotch Bonnets and tomatoes in the bowl of a food processor and process them into a thick paste. Place the tomato mixture and the onion, brine, vinegar, and allspice in a non-reactive saucepan. Bring to a boil, lower the heat to a simmer, and cook for about an hour, stirring frequently, until the juice is almost gone. Add the butter and cook until about the consistency of apple butter (which is the right consistency for bottling; about 10 minutes). Bottle in sterilized jars and seal.

NOTE: Prepare a 10% brine solution by dissolving 3 tablespoons of salt in 2 cups of water. The solution should allow a small egg to float.

*See "A Note about Yields" on page 137.

Devil Sauce   *Makes about 3 pints**

Gail's mother, Bo Arner, liked Mrs. MacCauley's sauce (see page 181) so much that she noodled around with it until she developed her own version, which is similar yet completely different in flavor.

16 Scotch Bonnet chillies, stemmed (see Note, page 120)
3½ pounds tomatoes (not too ripe), chopped
3 large red bell peppers, cored, seeded, and coarsely chopped
12 small onions, coarsely chopped
4 large cloves garlic, chopped
1 thumb-sized piece fresh ginger, crushed
1 stick cinnamon, broken up
12 whole allspice berries
1 teaspoon hot dry mustard powder
1 teaspoon Madras curry powder
1½ cups cane vinegar
1½ cups brine (see note)

Place the Scotch Bonnets, tomatoes, red peppers, onions, garlic, ginger, cinnamon, allspice, mustard, and curry powder in the bowl of a food processor, and process until the consistency is like course applesauce. (You may have to do this in several batches.) Combine this mixture with the vinegar and brine in a large, non-reactive pot. Bring to a boil, then reduce the heat and cook for 1 hour, stirring occasionally, until the juice is almost gone. Spoon the mixture into hot, sterilized jars and seal.

NOTE: Prepare a 10% brine solution by dissolving 3 tablespoons of salt in 2 cups of water. The solution should allow a small egg to float.

*See "A Note about Yields" on page 137.

ON THE SIDE

Pukka Sahib Anchovy Sauce   *Makes about 2 cups*

The British colonization of the Indian subcontinent transformed the English palate. It introduced those at home to the delicacies of sophisticated spices and a wide array of condiments, both
traditional to the subcontinent and the result of Anglo-Indian mixing. One such addition to the
British kitchen was this sauce. Fish-based sauces have been used in Europe on and off since the
ancient Romans delighted in *garum*. This anchovy-based sauce is not nearly as pungent but works
just fine when served with leftover lamb or cold roast beef.

¼ pound anchovies preserved in salt
3 cups dark ale
3 shallots, peeled and minced
½ cup sautéed mushrooms
½ teaspoon superfine sugar
½ teaspoon ground ginger
¼ teaspoon ground mace
Pinch of ground allspice
Pinch of ground cloves

Rinse the salt off of the anchovies and pat them dry with absorbent paper. Combine all the
ingredients in a medium non-reactive saucepan. Bring the mixture to a boil, then lower the
heat and allow it to simmer gently, uncovered, for 1 hour, or until the sauce has thickened and
reduced by a third. Remove the sauce from the heat, allow it to cool, and then strain it into
sterilized jars, cover, and refrigerate.

A MUSTARDLY DIGRESSION WITH A DOLLOP OF KETCHUP

Perhaps because it is so easy to cultivate, mustard is often overlooked by food scholars. In fact, it is a very old plant with an interesting history. Indus Valley civilizations used it to season meats as early as 2300 B.C. There are white, black, and brown mustards, each being native to a different region of the world. Mustards are relatives of cabbage, radishes, broccoli, and watercress. Indeed, the baby mustard greens that are a trendy, spicy salad ingredient, and the mature mustard greens that are stewed down to a low gravy in more than one Southern pot, are the leaves of the same plant.

The Romans most likely turned mustard seeds into a paste by mixing them with unfermented grape juice, vinegar, oil, and honey. They also used it as a pickling spice. The infamous Roman *garum*, a salty fermented fish sauce included mustard, as did *muria*, a less expensive version prepared sometimes with mustard and the brine drained from preserved tunafish. The tiny grains even find their way into the Christian Bible where the faithful are informed that faith as small as a grain of mustard seed can move mountains.

The Romans probably brought mustard to France where it was taken up with great zest, and by the thirteenth century the city of Dijon had become the mustard capital of France, a spot that it continues to hold to this day. Because of its ready availability and affordability compared to other ingredients, mustard became a popular spice and was found in households both rich and poor. By the nineteenth century, Messieurs Grey and Poupon went into partnership to produce the mustard that still bears their name. The original Grey Poupon factory still stands in Dijon, but the name is owned today by Nabisco.

The English loved their mustard as well and used it with dishes like brawn, a concoction similar to the South's headcheese. Tewkesbury mustard is even mentioned in Shakespeare's *Henry IV*; the town, though, no longer makes the condiment.

In the early twentieth century, Colman's, a British brand of mustard, invented the Mustard Club, a clever ad campaign featuring such characters as monocle-wearing Lord Bacon of Cookham, his consort, Lady Hearty, the rotund Baron de Beef, and the comely secretary Miss Di Gester. The campaign was a wild success and one of the early endeavors of author Dorothy Sayers, who detailed her exploits in the world of advertising in the Lord Peter Wimsey mystery novel *Death Must Advertise*.

Across the Atlantic, America's most famous mustard, French's, was introduced at the St. Louis World's Fair in 1904 along with the hot dog, to which it has become inextricably linked. It was first prepared by George French from mustard seed, salt, vinegar, and seasonings including turmeric, which gives it its characteristic yellow color.

Different cultures have different ways of preparing mustard. Mild, sweet versions predominate in Scandinavia, while the British like a hearty zap. Germany even can boast *Senf Meisters* (master mustard makers) who whip up their individualized specialties to serve up on the country's wursts. Italy's mustards can range from the familiar spread to the *mostarda di Cremona*: a fruit pickle of pears, apricots, cherries, plums, peaches, melons, and more, preserved in a syrup flavored with mustard oil.

In the cuisines of India, mustard seeds are often heated until they pop, which gives them a nutty flavor and removes some of the pungency. And anyone who has ever eaten Chinese mustard knows that it can literally take your breath away.

Americans have traditionally preferred a milder mustard like Mr. French's, but in recent years we've become omnivores, eating and enjoying all of the world's mustards. We even have a mustard museum to prove it: The Mount Horeb Mustard Museum, in Mount Horeb, Wisconsin.

KETCHUP

This tabletop condiment boasts a history almost as old as its yellow counterpart. The word *Ke-tsiap* or *kesiap* in the Amoy dialect of China referred to a popular seventeenth-century Chinese condiment that was a spicy pickled fish sauce. The word is considered to be the origin of our word ketchup, also spelled catsup and catchup. Others suggest, though, that the word may come from the Malay word *kechap* or *kejap* meaning soy sauce (today spelled *kecap)*. There are several different kinds of *kecap* in Southeast Asia, including *kecap manis*, a dark soy flavored with palm sugar and spices including star anise, coriander, and laos, the rhyzome of a plant of the ginger family. There are also *kecap asin*, a thinner, saltier version of the sauce, and *kecap ikan*, a fish sauce. Dutch traders and British sailors brought the word as well as the product to Europe, where ketchups were prepared with ingredients ranging from mushrooms to young fresh walnuts. Tomato ketchup is a later invention that many attribute to thrifty New England Yankees looking for another way to put up a bumper crop of tomatoes.

Ketchup, whether made with mushrooms, tomatoes, or cherries, is a smooth condiment that hovers between being thick enough to prevent separation and yet not so thick that it will not pour. In making ketchups, it is important to remember that they will thicken as they cool.

Mustard   *Makes about ⅓ cup*

It's not difficult to make your own mustard, and it can become rather habit-forming once you've managed it. Here's a basic recipe. You can vary the taste of the mustard by changing the vinegar and spices.

2 tablespoons brown mustard seeds
2 tablespoons white mustard seeds
¼ cup white wine vinegar (approximately)
½ teaspoon minced fresh tarragon, or to taste
Freshly ground white pepper, to taste

Grind the mustard seeds in a spice mill or mortar and pestle and place them in a medium glass jar with 1 tablespoon of water. Let stand for 1 hour, then add just enough of the vinegar to cover the seeds. Add the tarragon and pepper and stir to mix. Cover the jar and let it sit for a week in the refrigerator so the mustard can mature. After a week, drain off the excess liquid, seal the jar, and refrigerate for two weeks. The mustard will mature as you keep it, but it should be used quickly after first use.

Pineapple-Rum Mustard *Makes about ½ cup*

This hot, Caribbean-inspired mustard is based on the Champagne mustards of France. I came up with it for a show that I was doing with Sara Moulton on the Food Network in 1999.

2 tablespoons white mustard seeds
1 tablespoon brown mustard seeds
1½ tablespoons dry mustard powder
¼ cup fresh pineapple, finely minced
1 teaspoon fresh thyme leaves
Small pinch dried Scotch Bonnet chillies, or to taste
2 teaspoons Demerara sugar (see Note)
6 tablespoons or more dark rum (the amount will vary depending on the thickness desired)
Salt, to taste

Grind the mustard seeds in a mortar and pestle or spice mill. Place the ground mustard seeds in a bowl with enough water to moisten and allow them to sit for 10 minutes. Return the soaked seeds to the mortar or place in the bowl of a food processor with the mustard powder, pineapple, thyme, chillies, sugar, rum, and salt to taste. Pound or process until the desired consistency is reached. Pour off any excess liquid, then spoon the mustard into a small jar. Cover tightly and refrigerate. The mustard should sit for at least 2 weeks before use.

NOTE: Demerara sugar is a dry, coarse-textured raw sugar from Guyana. You can find it in specialty markets or online.

Mostarda di Frutta   *Makes about 4 cups*

This is a traditional Italian use of mustard. Perhaps the best known of these mustards is the *mostarda di Cremona* made with pears, cherries, peaches, and figs along with lemons and other fresh fruits in a syrup of mustard, white wine, and honey. *Mostarda di Veneto* uses quince or apples; *mostarda alla toscana* adds a bit of *vin santo* in a syrup of grape must. The *mostarda di frutta piccante* is the hottest one of all and uses puréed fruit. This simple variation is easy to make at home and is great with grilled meats, particularly poultry.

1½ cups sugar

⅓ pound nectarines, pitted and cut into bite-size pieces

⅓ pound apricots, pitted and cut into bite-size pieces

⅓ pound Santa Rosa plums, pitted and cut into bite-size pieces

½ cup balsamic vinegar

½ cup raspberry vinegar

2 teaspoons dry mustard powder

2 teaspoons yellow mustard seeds

⅓ pound California-style dried apricots, snipped into bite-size pieces

⅓ pound dried nectarines, snipped into bite-size pieces

⅓ pound dried Santa Rosa plums, pitted and cut into bite-size pieces

Place ¾ cup of the sugar in a medium saucepan with 1 cup of water, bring it to a boil, then lower the heat. Continue to cook, stirring frequently until you have a syrup. Add the fresh nectarines, apricots, and plums to the syrup and continue to simmer for 10 minutes, or until the fruit is tender. Combine the remaining ¾ cup of sugar in a medium non-reactive saucepan with the vinegars and mustards. Bring the mixture to a boil, then lower the heat and simmer for 5 minutes. Allow both syrups to cool to room temperature, then mix them together and add the dried apricots, nectarines, and plums. Spoon the fruit into sterilized jars, making sure that they are covered with the syrup, then seal and process (see page 103).

Cherry Ketchup   *Makes two 8-ounce jars*

I love cherries and cannot get enough of them in season. One year I purchased $50 worth before heading off to Martha's Vineyard, where cherries are even more expensive than in New York City. I found that my bumper crop was going bad by the third week and thought I'd better do something; this is what I came up with. If you want a smoother, more ketchup-like consistency, put the mixture through a sieve after cooking. Be careful not to overcook this ketchup; if you do, you'll have a cherry chutney. Remove it when it seems a bit too runny to be a ketchup. You'll need about a pound and a half of cherries for the pulp, but the exact amount will depend on how juicy your cherries are. This ketchup is great with grilled or roasted meats.

1½ pounds bing red cherries, pitted
⅓ cup plus 1 tablespoon cider vinegar
1 tablespoon jalapeño balsamic vinegar (page 193)
¾ cup sugar
¼ teaspoon ground ginger
Pinch of ground cinnamon
Pinch of freshly grated nutmeg

Prepare the cherry pulp by placing the pitted cherries in a food processor and pulsing until they become a thick paste. You want 2 cups of pulp. Combine the pulp, vinegars, sugar, ginger, cinnamon, and nutmeg in a non-reactive saucepan. Bring the mixture to a boil, lower the heat, and cook for about a half an hour, or until the mixture is almost the thickness of ketchup. Spoon into sterilized jars and seal.

Piquillo Ketchup   *Makes about 3 pints**

This recipe was sent to me by my friend Matt Rowley, who is a pickling fiend. He's adapted and updated a recipe from Ola Powell's *1918 Successful Canning and Preserving* for pimiento ketchup, using the Spanish *piquillo* pepper. The result is, as he pronounces it, "kick-ass." The peppers are available canned and give a flavor all their own to this ketchup. It's a grand addition to stews and soups, and can even be used as a sandwich spread.

4 pounds (drained weight) roasted Spanish *piquillo* chillies
1 tablespoon kosher salt
1½ pounds (3½ cups minus 2 tablespoons) sugar
1 to 2 tablespoons ground ginger
1 to 2 tablespoons ground cinnamon
3 cups cider vinegar

Grind the *piquillos* in a food processor to a slushy purée still with some pieces no bigger than grains of rice. Pour the purée into a large, non-reactive pot and mix in the salt, sugar, ginger, cinnamon, and vinegar. Bring the mixture to a boil, reduce to a simmer, and cook uncovered, stirring occasionally, until it reaches a ketchup like consistency, about 45 minutes. Pour the ketchup into sterilized jars, seal, cool, and refrigerate, or seal and process (see page 103).

SAVORY SAUCES AND OTHER ENHANCERS

*See "A Note about Yields" on page 137.

Nibbling Onions   *Serves 2*

This sinfully simple yet delicious recipe is again from Matt Rowley. The trick is in the sumac, a tart, lemony-tasting Middle Eastern spice that perks up the onions and makes them "nibbling" good.

1 large Vidalia or other sweet onion, thinly sliced
1 teaspoon sumac (see Note)

Place the onion slices in a small shallow bowl and sprinkle them liberally with the sumac. Cover with plastic wrap and allow them to sit for at least 1 hour. Serve at room temperature with grilled meats.

NOTE: See Mail Order Sources, page 199.

Jalapeño Balsamic Vinegar   *Makes 2 cups*

This almost-too-simple-to-be-a-recipe recipe adds flavor to everything it touches. It can spice up a soup or add a bit of zip to a salad dressing. It can even serve as a table condiment all by itself if dressed up in a fancy cruet.

10 jalapeño chillies, cut into ½-inch slices, or more to taste (see Note, page 120)
2 cups balsamic vinegar

Place the jalapeño slices into a wide mouthed jar and cover with the vinegar. Seal and allow it to sit for 1 week then serve as a table condiment. Pour out a bit of the peppery vinegar on whatever you wish. Those who want more "bite" can add the pickled jalapeños too.

Sherry Peppers   *Makes 1 cruet*

Outerbridge's makes these peppers in Bermuda where they are a must for the fish chowder. You can make your own variation without all of Outerbridge's secret ingredients, but with all of the fresh taste of the sherry. In keeping with Bermuda's style, make these directly in a glass cruet. Please remember, the better the sherry, the better the sherry peppers. This is not a recipe that requires very expensive sherry, but don't use so-called cooking sherry. A nice amontillado will be grand or, if you like it drier, a fino.

20 bird chillies, cleaned and stemmed (see Note, page 120)
1 bottle dry sherry

Poke the chillies into the cruet with your finger or a chopstick. Pour the sherry into the top. Drink 1 glass of the remaining sherry and then return it to your liquor cabinet. Seal the cruet and allow it to sit for a week. Add a few drops of the pepper liquid to the soup or stew of your choice.

Molho Brasileiro *Makes 1 cup*

I learned how to prepare this sauce in Brazil, where it goes with grilled meats and also with the greens known as *couve* that accompany *feijoada*, the national dish of Brazil. I find that the lemon-based sauce goes beautifully with pork and also mixes well with black beans and rice. It's sublime with greens in any form.

1 small onion, minced
1 tablespoon minced cilantro, or to taste
1 jalapeño chilli, minced, or to taste (see Note, page 120)
½ cup freshly squeezed lemon juice
2 tablespoons olive oil

Mix all of the ingredients together in a small bowl. Cover with plastic wrap and allow to sit for 1 hour. Serve with grilled meats.

Seagrape Jelly *Makes about 1½ pints*

My friend Gail McDonough spent time in Miami where she added this recipe to her repertoire. It's one of the most unusual condiments I've ever seen, so I include it here for those of you who live in coastal areas. As she puts it, "This recipe is unusual as it is the only recipe I have ever seen for the ubiquitous seagrape, the graceful tree growing on every beach from Miami to Venezuela." In her words,

> The Sausage Tree stand was an old Miami landmark. Mrs. Black started—in the '30s is my best guess—Depression era—to make ends meet in an area of Miami that was up until the early '60s still part farmland. It was located on the opposite side of Old Cutler Road from Matheson Hammock and Fairchild Tropical Garden in South Miami. There Mrs. Black sold jams and jellies and anything else she could, but by the time I knew her in the late '40s it was more a hobby and tradition than necessity. I used to ride my horse down there and she would feed me and the horse whatever she had baked. My horse also liked beer and BBQ, but that's another story.

Gail cautions, "It is important for the seagrape fruit to be a dark, leathery purple. If they are not ripe, the result will be horribly bitter."

4 cups strained seagrape juice
1 tablespoon freshly squeezed key lime juice
3 cups sugar

Heat the seagrape juice in deep, heavy jelly pan with a copper bottom. (We used the bottom of a pressure cooker.) Add the lime juice and sugar and stir until the sugar is dissolved. Boil on high heat until a candy thermometer reaches 225 degrees. Skim the jelly several times during cooking and watch the pot carefully so it doesn't boil over. Pour the jelly gently into hot sterilized jars, skim again, and cover with paraffin to seal.

ON THE SIDE

METRIC EQUIVALENCIES

LIQUID AND DRY MEASURE EQUIVALENCIES

Customary	Metric
¼ teaspoon	1.25 milliliters
½ teaspoon	2.5 milliliters
1 teaspoon	5 milliliters
1 tablespoon	15 milliliters
1 fluid ounce	30 milliliters
¼ cup	60 milliliters
⅓ cup	80 milliliters
½ cup	120 milliliters
1 cup	240 milliliters
1 pint (2 cups)	480 milliliters
1 quart (4 cups)	960 milliliters (.96 liter)
1 gallon (4 quarts)	3.84 liters
1 ounce (by weight)	28 grams
¼ pound (4 ounces)	114 grams
1 pound (16 ounces)	454 grams
2.2 pounds	1 kilogram (1000 grams)

OVEN-TEMPERATURE EQUIVALENCIES

Description	°Fahrenheit	°Celsius
Cool	200	90
Very slow	250	120
Slow	300–325	150–160
Moderately slow	325–350	160–180
Moderate	350–375	180–190
Moderately hot	375–400	190–200
Hot	400–450	200–230
Very Hot	450–500	230–260

MAIL ORDER SOURCES

Bajan Condiments and Hot Sauces
www.native-treasures.com

Cane Syrup, Cane Vinegar
Steen's
Steen's Syrup Mill
PO Box 339
Abbeville, LA 70510

1-800-725-1654
www.steensyrup.com

Chillies and Tropical Fruits
Frieda's by Mail
PO Box 58488
Los Angeles, CA 90058

1-800-241-1771
www.friedas.com

The Chile Guy
PO Box 1839
Bernalillo, NM 87004

1-800-869-9218
www.chileguy.com

Hispanic Products
Goya Foods
Available at Hispanic stores and in most
supermarkets

Middle Eastern Ingredients
Sahadi's Fine Foods
187 Atlantic Avenue
Brooklyn, NY 11235

1-718-624-4550
www.sahadis.com

***Pimentón* and Other Spices**
Dean & DeLuca
560 Broadway
New York, NY 10012

1-800-221-7714
www.deananddeluca.com

Spices and Spice Blends
Adriana's Caravan
78 Grand Central Terminal
New York, NY 10017

1-800-316-0820
www.adrianascaravan.com

MAIL ORDER SOURCES

Kalustyan's
123 Lexington Avenue
New York, NY 10016

1-800-352-3451
www.kalustyans.com

Penzeys
PO Box 933
Muskego, WI 53150

1-800-741-7787
www.penzeys.com

Vanns Spices
6105 Oakleaf Avenue
Baltimore, MD 21215

1-800-583-1693
www.vannsspices.com

Vinegars and Olive Oils
Zingerman's
422 Detroit Street
Ann Arbor, MI 48104

1-888-636-8162
www.zingermans.com

Canning Supplies
Alltrista Consumer Products Company
PO Box 2729
Muncie, IN 47307-0729
1-800-240-3340
www.homecanning.com

Makers of Ball and Kerr canning jars
1-800-392-2575

Home Canning Supply & Specialists
PO Box 1158WW
Ramona, CA 92065

1-760-788-0520

Index

INDEX

About the Author

Jessica B. Harris is one of a handful of African-Americans who have achieved prominence in the culinary world. Having received a doctorate at New York University, she teaches English at a college in New York and has contributed to *Cooking Light, Food & Wine, The New Yorker,* and other publications. She has spoken about food on morning talk shows and lectures on food around the country. She lives in New York when she can't be in New Orleans.